Based mostly upon the Apostle P(Christians in Romans 5-8, this sc illustrated 'take' on Christianity 1 clarity. Readers from 'teens' to 'nineties', will be uplifted and fascinated by this 'cat-scan' of our bold new identity and secure status in Christ, so we can live dazzlingly different lives.
Greg Haslam – Senior Pastor, Westminster Chapel, London

Jesus and the New Testament Apostles urge us to build our lives on right foundations.

So whether you are a new Christian exploring these truths for the first time - or have been following Jesus for years and just want to ensure you are still building aright - then this book is for you!

Andrew has served us well giving us clear biblical doctrine filled with fresh life experiences - helping all of us to continue to build our lives on the solid rock that is Jesus Christ!
Jeremy Simpkins – Leader of Christ Central Churches (Part of Newfrontiers)

This excellent study book covers all the major truths that we need to understand in order to be a mature and fruitful Christian. It does this in a way that is both thorough and accessible. I think it is essential reading for all Christians whether young or old in the faith.
John Groves – Bible Teacher and Church Leader

Really nothing is more important for Christians than to have a right understanding of themselves. That means having God's understanding of who we are. For the Apostle Paul the way he most frequently described a Believer was to say that they are, 'In Christ'. This book examines this description in a helpful and accessible way. Get hold of the truths expressed here and apply them to your own life and thinking and it really will make a radical difference to the way you see yourself, are able to stand firm in a crisis and also to live fruitfully for God.

John Hosier – **Author, Bible Teacher and Church Leader**

ANDREW BUNT

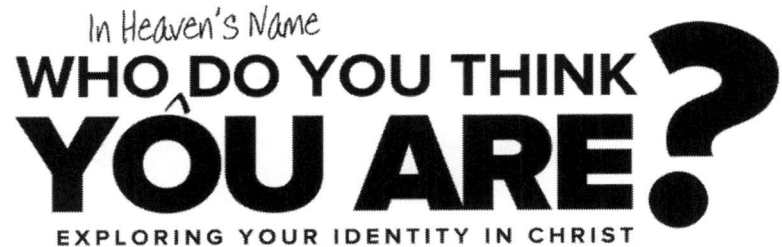

WHO IN HEAVEN'S NAME DO YOU THINK YOU ARE?

EXPLORING YOUR IDENTITY IN CHRIST

Copyright © 2014 Andrew Bunt

All rights reserved. No part of this publication may be reproduced, distributed or transmitted in any form or by any means, including photocopying, recording, or other electronic or mechanical methods, without the prior written permission of the publisher, except in the case of brief quotations embodied in critical reviews and certain other noncommercial uses permitted by copyright law.

Charis Books
Darlington, United Kingdom
info@charisbooks.co.uk

Book Layout © 2013 BookDesignTemplates.com
Cover Design by Harvey Appleton (www.harveyappleton.co.uk)

ISBN-13 978-1-4991-4113-9
ISBN-10 1-4991-4113-0

Unless otherwise indicated, all Scripture quotations are from The Holy Bible, English Standard Version® (ESV®), copyright © 2001 by Crossway Bibles, a publishing ministry of Good News Publishers. Used by permission. All rights reserved.

Scripture quotations marked NIV are from THE HOLY BIBLE, NEW INTERNATIONAL VERSION®, NIV® Copyright © 1973, 1978, 1984, 2011 by Biblica, Inc.® Used by permission. All rights reserved worldwide; NLT are taken from the Holy Bible, New Living Translation, copyright © 1996, 2004, 2007 by Tyndale House Foundation. Used by permission of Tyndale House Publishers, Inc., Carol Stream, Illinois 60188. All rights reserved; KJV are from the King James Version of the Bible (Public Domain); All emphases are added by the author.

For

King's Church Darlington

&

'My Little Darlo Family'

Contents

Preface	ix
Acknowledgements	xiii
Before You Get Started...	15
Introduction	19
1. You Are... Chosen	23
2. You Are... A New Creation	33
3. You Are... Free From Condemnation	41
4. You Are... Dead To Sin And Alive To God	55
5. You Are... Dead To The Law	65
6. You Are... Adopted	75
7. You Are... A Witness	87
8. You Are... A Member Of The Body Of Christ	97
9. You Are... A Temple Of The Holy Spirit	109
10. You Are... Part Of A Holy Priesthood	121
11. You Are... Salt And Light	129
12. You Are... A Fellow Sufferer	137
13. You Are... More Than A Conqueror	145
Group Study Guides	157

Preface

The journey which has culminated in the writing of this book began three years ago, in a restaurant in Darlington town centre. The meal was to mark my last evening in Darlington, where I had been working for King's Church for a year, before I was to move to Durham ready to begin my studies at the university. At that meal Jonathan Lloyd, whose house I had lived in that year and who is an elder at King's, turned to me and told me about an idea he had had for the next Sunday morning teaching series at King's, all about our identity as Christians. I remember vividly how disappointed I was that I wouldn't be around to be involved in the series. Little did I know that God would use that idea to shape the next few years of my life.

Jonathan kept me up to speed as plans for the series developed, and as the months went by it became apparent that there was an important role I could play in making the series something that could really benefit the church. Alongside other things, God used this opportunity to bring me back to Darlington for the subsequent years of my degree. Throughout the series I produced guides to the relevant biblical passages to serve our mid-week small group leaders. When the series came to an end I started work on this book, and two years later the whole project has finally reached its conclusion. The release of this book comes at the point when I move on from Darlington to a new location and new phase of life, but I will always look back on these years with fondness and gratitude for how God used them to shape me. It's amazing what God can bring out of a simple conversation over dinner.

***

I've dedicated this book to two groups of people who have played an important part in my life throughout this project.

First, to King's Church Darlington. In my four years at King's I have been privileged to have been given opportunities which go far beyond what is common for individuals of my age and to have been given the freedom to discover and develop my gifting. Thank you to Phil and the eldership team for the opportunities you have given me and to everyone at King's for your friendship, support and encouragement. As I move on it is my prayer that each one of you would come to understand the truths expounded in this book more and more and see them make an ever increasing difference in your lives.

The second group of people to whom this book is dedicated is 'my little Darlo Family', a small group of amazing people who have taken me into their lives, their homes and their families.

First, the Myers family. Nathan and Anneliese, thank you for everything. You have shown me what it is to be a single who lives in family. Thank you for loving me, standing by me through highs and lows and for giving me the privilege of being involved in your children's lives. Words can't express the impact you've had on my life, and even though we will soon be many miles apart, I will continue to consider you my family. Make sure, wherever you might end up, that you have a spare room. I will be using it!

Elliot, Carys – who continues to make me consider myself the luckiest godfather in the world – and Lydia, thank you for sharing your toys with me, helping me switch off from my studies and giving me lots of love. God has used you to teach me something about how he feels about his children. I pray that each one of you will grow to know the truths discussed in this book as realities in your own lives.

Second, the Ward family. Steve and Becky, I don't know what to say. Perhaps the best that words can do is to say that I am truly a different man today because of the love and support you have given me over the past four years. No one else has ever tried so hard to understand the ups and downs of the path on which God has put me. You've taken me into your family and stuck by me in good times and bad. You've walked with me through some of the darkest days of my life and given me some of my happiest memories. I don't know what God has planned for me or for you in the coming years, but I do know that my move down South isn't the end of our friendship. Who knows, maybe one day we'll end up planting that church after all?

Richard, Catherine (and Emma!), thank you for sharing your parents with me, and for your friendship. Your love and acceptance have been a great source of strength and encouragement for me. I count myself lucky to have you as my brother and sisters.

Acknowledgements

Writing a book is no small task. Many people have helped and encouraged me along the way and I owe a deep debt of gratitude to them all. A few should be mentioned by name.

First, Jonathan Lloyd, who came up with the idea for the preaching series from which this book grew and has been a constant source of encouragement to keep going with what became a very long project. He and his wife Fran have kindly let me live in their home for the past four years, which has proved a wonderful environment for me both personally and in regard to my studies. Thank you both for your help with this project and everything else you have done for me over these years. I will deeply miss living with you but look forward to visiting for many years to come.

Though this book grew out of a teaching series given at King's Church Darlington in the spring and summer of 2012, most of the material is my own fresh take on these topics. I owe the basic ideas of the introduction and chapter 7, however, to Jonathan.

Several people read extracts of the text and gave useful feedback. Thanks to Ken and Louise Snider, Shereen Kipling and Ben Ingall. Special thanks must go to Edwin Pugh who gave his time to read the entire manuscript, despite never having even met the author, and gave incredibly useful feedback which greatly improved the finished product. Both my parents have also read some or all of the text and given useful feedback and encouragement. Thank you for your continued support in everything I do.

My dear friend Harvey Appleton has done a fantastic job on the cover design. Thank you for that and your continued friendship.

Finally, I must thank the person who has done more than anyone else to shape this book and to encourage me to actually finish it: Jill Jackson. Jill's ideas and perceptive comments have helped a young academic write something that will hopefully be accessible and enjoyable for any Christian, as well as providing encouragement and advice throughout the process. Thank you Jill. I hope you are pleased with the finished product!

Before You Get Started...

Most books don't feel the need to give their readers tips about how to read them, but this book isn't like most books. *Who In Heaven's Name Do You Think You Are?* isn't just about reading; it's about finding out who you really are as a Christian and thinking through how you can live out that identity.

Each of the chapters that follow is designed to help you move from reading to understanding and then to living. At the end of each there is an *Identity Check-Up* section which contains three different features to help you do this:

Understanding Your Identity

In this section you'll find questions designed to help you really get to grips with the passage of the Bible the chapter has been discussing. The Bible is where God has told us who we are as Christians so we need to open it, dig into it and try to understand what it says. These questions will help you do that. If you're reading the book on your own you can just take some time to think about them; if you're reading with one or two others, discuss the questions together and see if you can learn from each other. If you're using *Who In Heaven's Name Do You Think You Are?* as the basis for a study in a larger group where not everyone has read the relevant chapter, you might want to replace these questions with the Group Study Guides discussed below.

Living Your Identity

These questions help you move from understanding the biblical truth to applying it to your daily life, so it makes a difference to the way you live. Again you can think about these on your own, with a friend or two or in a larger group.

Growing In Your Identity

Here you'll find something to do or to pray about which aims at helping you apply the biblical truth to your life in the longer term. This section is designed for individuals but could still work for a group setting.

Using *Who In Heaven's Name Do You Think You Are?* In A Group

If you're in a bigger group, using the book as the basis for discussions where not everyone is reading the chapters, you might want to take a different approach to exploring the biblical passage. At the end of the book you can find Group Study Guides for each chapter, designed especially to help you use it in such contexts.

Bible Translations

Who In Heaven's Name Do You Think You Are? uses a few different Bible translations. The question of which Bible translation someone should use is not really about which translation is best as much as it is about what you want to do with it. For that reason the passages at the beginning of each chapter are given in the *English Standard Version* because it is a fairly literal translation and makes it easier for us to explore in the rest of the chapter what the original writer was saying. The downside of this is that sometimes these passages can be a little hard to understand on a first reading. Let me encourage you to read the biblical passage before you read the chapter and then keep referring to it as you read the text because the whole point of what follows is to explain that passage. Hopefully if you read the biblical passage through again after reading the chapter it will make a lot more sense. If it helps, you might also want to have another translation (such as the *New Living Translation*) with you while you read.

Bible verses quoted in the chapters come from a variety of translations – whichever communicates the meaning most clearly. You'll find a note of the translation in brackets after the quote.

The Group Study Guides are based on the *English Standard Version* but are also aware of the *New International Version* and *New Living Translation*. It is hoped that this will make the guides easier to use in a group setting.

Introduction

Who we are is important. We spend our lives building and protecting an identity. Who we are affects everything: what we do, what we say, who we spend our time with, where we go, how we feel about ourselves, how we deal with difficult times and how we think about the future. All of these are affected by our understanding of our identity.

A lot of people go through life searching to find out who they really are. Some people do so by going travelling to 'discover themselves'; others cling to their family heritage or, in some cases, try to get as far away from it as possible. Some people try to build their identity on their career, relationships or material possessions. But none of these things can really reveal who we are.

God tells us that we are his image bearers – that's the first thing he says about us (Genesis 1:26-27). We were made to live in relationship with him, being his representatives on the earth. So if we want to know who we really are, we've got to explore who we are in relation to him.

A New Birth Certificate

One time when Jesus was in Jerusalem for the Passover, he was approached by a man called Nicodemus (John 3:1-15). Nicodemus was 'a man of the Pharisees'. The Pharisees were people who were obsessed with keeping the minute details of the law. They had taken the laws of the Old Testament and added loads of oral tradition about how they should be kept to make sure they didn't accidentally fail to keep them.

Nicodemus comes to Jesus to ask him who he is, because he doesn't understand how Jesus is doing everything that people are reporting about him. Jesus tells him that 'unless one is born again he cannot see the kingdom of God' (John 3:3). This confuses Nicodemus: 'How can a man be born when he is old?' he asks (John 3:4). Jesus tells him, 'Unless one is born of water and the Spirit, he cannot enter the kingdom of God' (John 3:5). He's saying that keeping the law, even with all the effort of a Pharisee, won't get him into God's people, restored to the relationship he was made for.

To enter the kingdom, Jesus says, you have to be born again. That's a big thing. It's about a fresh start and a new identity. When you're born as a baby you're given a birth certificate which states your identity. Your birth certificate says who you are, who your parents are and where you were born. When you enter God's kingdom by being born again, you get a new identity, like getting a new birth certificate.

Playing In The Slum

But the problem is, if we don't know about this new identity it can't make any difference to our lives. We could have the best family heritage and be heir to a fortune, but if we don't know that, it won't make any difference to us. That's why, as Christians, we need to know our identity.

C.S. Lewis said that if we don't know our true identity as Christians we end up being 'half-hearted creatures fooling around with drink and sex and ambition when infinite joy is offered us, like an ignorant child who wants to go on making mud pies in a slum because he cannot imagine what is meant by the offer of a holiday at the sea'.[a]

We all need to open the Bible and let God explain who he has made us to be. Only then will we be able to enjoy the fullness of life Jesus came to give us (John 10:10).

The Riches Of His Glorious Inheritance

The Apostle Paul, one of the men commissioned by Jesus to establish the Church, took up this theme in his letter to the Ephesians. After a magnificent hymn of praise and thanks to God for the vast array of spiritual blessings poured out on Christians (Ephesians 1:3-14) he prays that the Ephesian believers would come to see what God has got for them now and in the future.

> [16] I have not stopped thanking God for you. I pray for you constantly, [17] asking God, the glorious Father of our Lord Jesus Christ, to give you spiritual wisdom and insight so that you might grow in your knowledge of God. [18] I pray that your hearts will be flooded with light so that you can understand the confident hope he has given to those he called—his holy people who are his rich and glorious inheritance.
>
> Ephesians 1:16-18 (NLT)

Paul prays that God would reveal to the Ephesians the present blessings of their identity and the certain hope they have for the future. We need to come with the same desire and prayer as we explore our identity in Christ. We will only really grasp all that God has for us if we let him work in us.

---

[a] C.S. Lewis, *The Weight of Glory* (S.P.C.K., 1942).

Identity Theft

It is these things, our very identity in Christ, which we are going to explore. But there's one more reason why this is so important. We don't just run the risk of missing out from not knowing our identity; we also have an enemy who is seeking to rob us of this identity.

The devil can't actually change who we are once we've been born again (1 John 5:18) but he loves to make us miss out on what God has for us now, by skewing our understanding of that identity and making us believe lies about ourselves.

Peter warned the Christians he wrote to 'Stay alert! Watch out for your great enemy, the devil. He prowls around like a roaring lion, looking for someone to devour. Stand firm against him, and be strong in your faith' (1 Peter 5:8-9 NLT).

We need to be ready to resist the lies of the devil and need to be firm in our faith to do so, knowing the truth with which to respond to his lies. If we are secure in our identity as Christians he won't be able to do anything to take that from us.

CHAPTER 1

You Are... Chosen

³Blessed be the God and Father of our Lord Jesus Christ, who has blessed us in Christ with every spiritual blessing in the heavenly places, ⁴even as he chose us in him before the foundation of the world, that we should be holy and blameless before him. In love ⁵he predestined us for adoption as sons through Jesus Christ, according to the purpose of his will, ⁶to the praise of his glorious grace, with which he has blessed us in the Beloved.
Ephesians 1:3-6

The Value Of Being Chosen

Everyone loves being chosen because being chosen is a statement of value. The little green aliens in *Toy Story* know that. They live in an arcade game at Pizza Planet ruled by the mysterious, god-like figure, The Claw. The Claw is a mechanical hand which descends into the mass of aliens and chooses one to leave when someone plays the game. Each time The Claw picks someone, the chosen toy is immediately honoured by the others as 'The Chosen One' while they look on in awe and wonder. The aliens know that being chosen is a statement of value.

A Sudden Outburst

Have you ever been so excited or so thankful that you've suddenly burst out in speech or maybe even into song? Perhaps you let out a cry when your team scored the winning goal or when you got your perfect job?

Well that's what Paul does in his letter to the Ephesians. Having started the letter, saying who he is and greeting those he's writing to, he opens with a great song of praise to God for all the blessings he's poured out on us as Christians. You can hear the passion in Paul and sense this song suddenly bursting out of him as if he can't contain it any more.

Every Spiritual Blessing In Christ

Ephesians 1:3 is a great place for us to start our exploration of who we are, because it's Paul's introduction to a passage in which he does exactly that. Paul praises God because of all the blessings he's poured out on us. In fact, it's not even just that God has given us a lot or something particularly good; it's that God has given us 'every spiritual blessing in the heavenly places' (Ephesians 1:3). God has poured out on us every spiritual blessing he could, and that leads Paul to thank, praise and worship him. As we look at who God has made us to be, the same reaction will grow in our hearts. The great number of blessings that God has poured out on us should lead us to thank him and worship him more and more.

Paul also tells us something else about these blessings. He says that they are for those who are 'in Christ'. 'In Christ' is a common phrase in Paul's letters which we'll look at in more detail later on (in *You Are... Free From Condemnation*), but it's worth quickly looking at it now because it will help us understand so much of what we are going to look at.

In his letter to the church in Rome, Paul explains that God sees all people as either 'in Adam' (the first man – Genesis 2) or 'in Christ' (Romans 5:12-19). Adam and Christ are the figureheads for two groups of people. All the people who are in Adam's group receive everything that Adam deserves for his actions, while all the people in Christ's group receive everything that Christ deserves. When we become Christians we are taken out of Adam's group and become members of Christ's group. That means that now we are Christians, God doesn't treat us in light of Adam's actions but in light of Christ's. So when Paul tells us we have been blessed 'in Christ with every spiritual blessing' (Ephesians 1:3), he means that we receive all these spiritual blessings because God has put us in Christ's group. We don't deserve them and couldn't deserve them, but Jesus does, and because we are in him they are given to us.

Chosen For A Purpose

The first of the spiritual blessings that Paul mentions is that God 'chose us in him [Christ] before the foundation of the world, that we should be holy and blameless before him' (Ephesians 1:4).

Paul tells us here that all Christians were chosen by God. The only reason anyone becomes a Christian is that God chose them. That's a big thing to get our heads around, and sometimes it raises questions in our minds which we can't answer. But in the Bible God makes it clear that he chose us. We are special to him and one of the great blessings he has given us is choosing us as those he would bless in the first place.

God made this choice 'before the foundation of the world' (Ephesians 1:4). If that's so, it tells us an important fact about it: God made it completely on his own. If it was before the world was even made, it couldn't have been because of anything we had done because we hadn't done anything yet. God chose you, as Paul goes on to say, purely because he loves you and wanted you to be in relationship with him and receive his blessings.

But what was this choice about? What were we chosen for? To be 'holy and blameless before him' (Ephesians 1:4). Holiness is about being set apart and devoted to God. There are two layers of meaning in 'holy and blameless', both of which we will explore more later. First, we are made 'holy and blameless' through the forgiveness that comes to us because of Jesus' sacrificial death for us. When we look at *You Are... Free From Condemnation* we will see how our position in Christ's group (being 'in Christ') is the way God sees us as worthy to be in relationship with himself.

Second, we are chosen to be 'holy and blameless' in the sense that once we become Christians, God's Spirit works in us to help us live holy lives. He gives us the freedom and the power to live the way he wants us to, which is the way we were made to live. This is sometimes called sanctification – a process of being sanctified or made holy. In this lifetime we will never reach the end of the journey, but when Jesus returns and we live with him in the New Creation we will finally be fully transformed into 'holy and blameless' individuals, living the life God designed us for.

Chosen In Love For Adoption

The next blessing Paul talks about also includes a reference to the fact that God has chosen us. 'In love he predestined us for adoption as sons through Jesus Christ, according to the purpose of his will, to the praise of his glorious grace, with which he has blessed us in the Beloved' (Ephesians 1:4-6).

Here Paul uses the word 'predestined', which is why God's choosing of Christians is sometimes called 'predestination'. To predestine simply means to make a set decision in advance. Here it means that God chose, before the foundation of the world, those who would become Christians and be adopted by him (which we'll discuss later in *You Are... Adopted*).

It's important to notice not just the truth being presented to us here but also how the Bible responds to that truth and the clues it gives us as to how it should make a difference in our lives. These verses give us a couple of these clues.

First we are told that it was 'in love' that God predestined us to be his. The fact that God chose us to be his and to be adopted by him, not because of anything we had done but purely out of his own choice, is an amazing proof of his deep love for us. Being chosen is always a statement of value. We all remember those times in school when teams were being picked for sport. Everyone wanted to be chosen because to be chosen is a statement of value. The same is true when God chooses us. What's even more amazing is that we were completely undeserving of being chosen and God was completely free not to choose us and yet, in love, he decided to do so. This isn't just like being picked first for the sports team. It's like being picked first even though everyone knows you'll be the worst player on the pitch.

We might be tempted at this point to ask why God would love us. In Deuteronomy we find Moses talking to the Israelites (God's people whom he had rescued from slavery in Egypt through the Exodus), and one of the things he reminds them is that they have been chosen by God.

Back in the New Testament, Peter, another of the first leaders of the Church, applies this Old Testament idea to Christians, calling us 'a chosen race' (1 Peter 2:9). What Moses says to the Israelites in Deuteronomy gives us a little insight into how we should think about God's choice to love us:

> ⁶For you are a holy people, who belong to the LORD your God. Of all the people on earth, the LORD your God has chosen you to be his own special treasure. ⁷The LORD did not set his heart on you and choose you because you were more numerous than other nations, for you were the smallest of all nations! ⁸Rather, it was simply that the LORD loves you.
>
> Deuteronomy 7:6-8 (NLT)

Moses reminds the Israelites that they are God's chosen people and then tells them that the reason God chose them and 'set his heart' on them was not because of anything they had done but because 'the LORD loves' them (Deuteronomy 7:7-8). Moses actually says the reason that God loves them is because he loves them! You could turn your nose up at that and say it's avoiding the question, but when you think about it, it's amazing. God doesn't love you because of anything you've done or will do. He doesn't love you because anything in you or about you makes you better than anyone else. He doesn't even love you because he has to. God loves you because he loves you. It's an unquestionable fact. It just is. And the glorious thing about that is that nothing we do can change it.

So when we think about the fact that God has chosen us, rather than getting bogged down in questions we can't answer, we should see the evidence of God's great love for us. Next time you're feeling unloved, unworthy or alone, remember that if you're a Christian, God chose you because he loves you, because he loves you, because he loves you...

To The Praise Of His Glorious Grace

Paul gives us another hint as to how we should respond to this truth and the difference it should make to our lives. He says that we were predestined for adoption 'to the praise of his glorious grace, with which he has blessed us in the Beloved' (Ephesians 1:6).

God choosing and adopting us is part of his grace given to us. Grace is an undeserved gift. We bring nothing to the table but God gives us everything.

Paul says that we are chosen and adopted in order that God might be praised and worshipped for this glorious grace. God's free choice of us demonstrates his loving, gracious nature and should lead us to worship him.

The two great themes throughout Paul's song in Ephesians 1 are that God has given us every blessing because he chose to, according to his will, and that this was so that he would be praised and worshipped.

We can sometimes think that reading the Bible is about finding out how to live and how to be 'good Christians'. There's some truth to this – as new creations and slaves to righteousness we want to live God's way out of love for him – but the Bible offers us so much more. When we get into God's Word we find there's a great inexhaustible bank of truth and good news. Often the first application, so easy to miss, is to recognise what God has done for us and to thank, praise and worship him.

Being chosen is definitely one such reason to praise God!

Identity Check-Up

Here are some questions and activities to help you perform an identity check-up.

Understanding Your Identity

Read Ephesians 1:3-6 and think about these questions.
- What does it mean to be 'in Christ'? How do we receive 'every spiritual blessing'?
- Look through the whole of Paul's song in Ephesians 1:3-14. What are the recurring themes?
- What was God's plan for us when he chose us? (vv.4-5)
- What was God's ultimate purpose in choosing us? (v.6)

Living Your Identity

Take some time to think about these questions or discuss them with others.
- Paul's song tells us that God chose us and made his plan for us with the ultimate goal that he would be worshipped. How does this differ from what you might have previously believed?
- How does knowing God chose you make you feel?
- How does Paul respond to the truth that we are chosen by God? What can we learn from the way he responds?

- What impact should this truth make in our lives day by day? How can we help it make a difference to us?

Growing In Your Identity

Paul knew the truths he writes about in Ephesians 1 so well and in such a real way that they caused praise to bubble out of him like an uncontrollable spring. God wants the same for us. Exploring our identity as Christians is pointless if it's just about learning more. God doesn't want us just to learn more about him but to experience him more. With each truth we are going to explore we need to make the effort and take the time to let it really soak in to us and make a difference so that it affects the way we live and leads us to worship God.

One way we can pursue this is by praying through passages of the Bible or meditating on them. All this means is reading them slowly, reminding ourselves what they really say, and proclaiming the truth to ourselves until it becomes deeply embedded within us.

Take some time to pray through and meditate on the following passages and let the truth they contain stir your heart. Spend some time thanking God for choosing you and worship him.

- Deuteronomy 7:6-8
- John 15:12-17
- Ephesians 1:3-6

CHAPTER 2

You Are... A New Creation

¹⁴For the love of Christ controls us, because we have concluded this: that one has died for all, therefore all have died; ¹⁵and he died for all, that those who live might no longer live for themselves but for him who for their sake died and was raised.

¹⁶From now on, therefore, we regard no one according to the flesh.ᵃ Even though we once regarded Christ according to the flesh, we regard him thus no longer. ¹⁷Therefore, if anyone is in Christ, he is a new creation. The old has passed away; behold, the new has come.

2 Corinthians 5:14-17

An Extreme Makeover

One of my friends used to like a TV programme called *Extreme Makeover*. The British version of *Extreme Makeover* was fairly standard. Like many other makeover shows, a deserving

---

ᵃ That is, 'from a human point of view' (NLT).

homeowner went away for a few days while their house was done up by a team of builders and decorators. The American version, however, took things a little further. Rather than just giving the existing house a lick of paint, some new wall art and possibly an extra room, in the American version the team would completely knock down the old house and build the family a new one. When they came back what they found was a totally new house. The old had gone and the new had come.

Every Christian is a new creation. We're not just some makeover job, given a bit of a clean-up. We are completely new creations. In one of his letters to the church in Corinth, Paul tells us about our status as new creations and what that means for us now.

A Change In View And A Change In State

In the early chapters of 2 Corinthians the Apostle Paul is defending himself from criticisms and challenges which have been brought against him. He concludes his self-defence by arguing that regardless of what people might be saying about him, he is always working for God and for the good of others. Why is this? 'For the love of Christ controls us, because we have concluded this: that one has died for all, therefore all have died; and he died for all, that those who live might no longer live for themselves but for him who for their sake died and was raised' (2 Corinthians 5:14-15). Paul has seen the love of Christ revealed in what he has done for Christians. Christ died and so in God's eyes those who are 'in Christ', in his group, have also died and are enabled to live a new life dedicated to God. This idea of dying with Christ and living a new life is important for our identity and is something we will come back to later. The important thing here is that when Paul saw God's love for him – displayed in the death and resurrection of Jesus – it completely transformed how he viewed his life and how he viewed other people.

Paul now goes on to explain some of the consequences of what he now understands. First he says that 'From now on, therefore, we regard no one according to the flesh' (2 Corinthians 5:16). What Jesus has done, the new life and new outlook he has given Paul, have shown him that outward appearances aren't important. It's the spiritual reality that is key.

This leads straight into the next result of Jesus' death and resurrection which is itself a new way of seeing people: 'Therefore if anyone is in Christ, new creation!'[b] (2 Corinthians 5:17). Paul doesn't use a verb – I think he said it something like that, with an implied 'wow' at the end. The focus is definitely on people, though, so that means *we* are this new creation. Just to really solidify his point, Paul explains, 'The old has passed away; behold, the new has come' (2 Corinthians 5:17).

New Creation

But what does it mean to say we are new creations? Most of us still look the same after we become Christians, so what's Paul on about? To understand what he means we've got to explore a bit more of the big story of God's plan for his creation.

God created a perfect world in which he placed human beings as his masterpiece, with the intention that they would live in perfect relationship with him, each other and the world, forever (Genesis 1-2). Sadly all that went pear-shaped when Adam and Eve, the first humans, rebelled against God by eating from the

---

[b] Author's translation.

Tree of the Knowledge of Good and Evil, directly disobeying what God had told them. Judgement had to follow, and the perfect relationships God had intended were destroyed. Humans were no longer in relationship with God, their relationships with each other would become difficult and they would no longer dwell in God's place, the Garden of Eden, or find it easy to work the land (Genesis 3). But God didn't leave it like this. It's always been his plan to repair the damage caused by this disaster, and that's the story the rest of the Bible tells.

As we move through the Bible we discover that God's ultimate plan is to make a new creation, where everything that went wrong in Eden is repaired and people will once again be in perfect relationship with him. The prophet Isaiah, one of God's messengers to his people in the Old Testament, saw this. After giving a warning that God's judgement would soon come upon his people because of their rebellion, he then promises that God will bring salvation and rescue them. Isaiah reports this message from God:

> For behold, I create new heavens
> and a new earth,
> and the former things shall not be remembered
> or come into mind.

Isaiah 65:17

This is the concept in Paul's mind when he talks about new creation. It's God's promise that at the end of time he will create new heavens and a new earth where there is no pain or suffering or sadness but where the vision of perfection seen in Eden is restored. So to say that we are 'new creations' is to say that in some sense we have already entered that coming new creation.

We are the first little bits of God's perfect, renewed creation breaking into history!

Seeing It The Way God Does

But it's still easy for us to question if we can really see this. That's why it's so important to look at things with spiritual eyes, as Paul has said in the previous verse.

We are new creations. Fact. We need to recognise that, believe it about ourselves and step into it.

What we think really does matter. How you think and how you view yourself will shape the way you feel and act. It's not about saying something often enough so that we convince ourselves it's true even if it isn't; it's about stepping into who we really are.

Being a new creation also tells us something about what it means to become a Christian. Becoming a Christian isn't about trying to be a good person or getting your ticket to heaven and sitting politely in the departure lounge until your time comes and you can finally escape. Becoming a Christian is being completely transformed, remade and renewed, ready for an eternity in God's new creation. It's not a botch job where God has given you a little wipe down to get some of the muck off; it's a completely new life. If you are a Christian, you are a new creation: God has totally transformed you!

Another thing being a new creation tells us about becoming a Christian is that we're part of something eternal, an eternity that starts now. Being a new creation reminds us that one day God will renew everything and we will live on his perfect new earth. It's a reminder to lift our eyes from the trouble of this world to the joy that's set before us. But it's also a reminder that this life and this world aren't all bad. We are new creations *now*. We live in relationship with God now and can experience something of what is coming in the future here in the present. We can enjoy life with God *now!*

So if you are 'in Christ', you are a new creation. The old has gone and the new has come.

Identity Check-Up

Here are some questions and activities to help you perform an identity check-up.

Understanding Your Identity

Read 2 Corinthians 5:14-17 and think about these questions.
- What has Paul come to understand according to vv.14-15?
- In what ways has this changed the way he looks at the world? (v.16)
- Where does the idea of 'new creation' come from and why is it important? (v.17; also Genesis 1-3; Isaiah 65:17-25; Revelation 21:1-22:5)

Living Your Identity

Take some time to think about these questions or discuss them with others.
- Is this how you tend to think of what happened to you when you became a Christian? If not, why not?
- What does the idea of being a 'new creation' tell you about what it means to be a Christian?
- How does being a 'new creation' shape our view of the future?

- How can we live in the light of this truth each day?

Growing In Your Identity

Grab a piece of paper and draw a line to divide it in half, creating two columns, one entitled 'Old Creation' and the other 'New Creation'. In the 'Old Creation' column write or draw as many things as you can think of that were true about you before you became a Christian. In the 'New Creation' column write or draw what is true of you now, as a Christian. They might be things that apply to all Christians (such as the many truths we'll be exploring through this book) or they might be specific to your own life story.

Spend some time thanking God that the old has gone and the new has come. You might want to keep your piece of paper handy so you can add to it as you come across more relevant changes throughout the course of the book.

CHAPTER 3

You Are... Free From Condemnation

There is therefore now no condemnation for those who are in Christ Jesus.
Romans 8:1

[12] Therefore, just as sin came into the world through one man, and death through sin, and so death spread to all men because all sinned— [13] for sin indeed was in the world before the law was given, but sin is not counted where there is no law. [14] Yet death reigned from Adam to Moses, even over those whose sinning was not like the transgression of Adam, who was a type of the one who was to come.

[15] But the free gift is not like the trespass. For if many died through one man's trespass, much more have the grace of God and the free gift by the grace of that one man Jesus Christ abounded for many. [16] And the free gift is not like the result of that one man's sin. For

the judgment following one trespass brought condemnation, but the free gift following many trespasses brought justification. [17]For if, because of one man's trespass, death reigned through that one man, much more will those who receive the abundance of grace and the free gift of righteousness reign in life through the one man Jesus Christ.

[18]Therefore, as one trespass led to condemnation for all men, so one act of righteousness leads to justification and life for all men. [19]For as by the one man's disobedience the many were made sinners, so by the one man's obedience the many will be made righteous.
Romans 5:12-19

One For All

Do you remember those times back in school when someone did something wrong but since no one would own up everyone got punished until they did? "If no one will admit to putting the frog in Mrs Lake's drawer everyone will lose their break times and lunchtimes until someone does!" I think the idea was that enough children would know who actually did it, so the social pressure upon them would force a confession. Looking back now it conjures up wonderful ideas of mafia-style mobs of children waiting for the individual outside the sweet shop at the end of the day. I'm not really convinced it works. Unless you happened to be in a class with the kids from *Bugsy Malone*, you were probably fairly safe. When someone finally confessed, whether they were the real culprit or not, everyone else was excused.

In such cases the actions of one individual have an effect on a whole group of people. The individuals are like representatives for the group. What should be happening to them happens to all.

I'm not sure Paul would have recognised our classroom stresses, but he uses a very similar idea when he's telling us about part of our identity in his letter to the Christians in Rome.

It All Goes Wrong

Right from the start humans have faced the problem of condemnation. When Adam and Eve sinned in the Garden of Eden by breaking God's command they were considered guilty; they came under condemnation and had to face the punishment (Genesis 3). God spoke curses over Adam and Eve and sent them out of the Garden forever (Genesis 3:23-24). Sin was followed by condemnation and condemnation was followed by punishment.

In Romans, Paul starts by explaining the condition which we all find ourselves in because of what happened in Eden. 'The wrath of God is revealed from heaven against all ungodliness and unrighteousness of men, who by their unrighteousness suppress the truth' (Romans 1:18). God's just anger against sin ('wrath') is on those who rebel against him. He links their wrongdoing ('unrighteousness') with that fact they 'suppress the truth'.

If we look at the events in Eden we find this is the root of the first sin too. God tells Adam and Eve that they're not to eat from the Tree of the Knowledge of Good and Evil 'for in the day that you eat of it you shall surely die' (Genesis 2:17). When the serpent comes along he lies to Eve, promising her she won't die from eating the fruit (Genesis 3:4). Eve believes the lie and her suppression of the truth leads her to sin.

In Romans, Paul explains his statement by telling us that something of who God is – 'his invisible attributes' – is obvious 'in the things that have been made', and because of this all people are 'without excuse' (Romans 1:20). In some way, God's reality is obvious and unavoidable when we look around us. Think of the vast expanse of the Sahara. That vitality of the Amazonian rainforest. The complexity of each part of our bodies. The beauty of art and music. The Dumbo octopus and the Glaucus Atlanticus (seriously, Google them!). Yet we all start by ignoring God. We know he's there but we don't respond to that fact as we should, by giving him our worship. Instead we 'exchanged the truth about God for a lie and worshiped and served the creature rather than the Creator' (Romans 1:25).

It's tempting for us to think this refers to someone else but not to ourselves. We don't worship creatures, we think. We've never bowed down to some statue or sacrificed an animal to some golden image. But even if we haven't done that, we will have given our primary devotion to something other than God. It might be money, work, other people or even just ourselves. We all fail to acknowledge who God is and to worship him as he deserves. We've all suppressed the truth of who God is and often even just the very fact that he's there.

What happens to us when we do this? 'The wrath of God is revealed' (Romans 1:18). God's just anger burns against us. We are guilty. We are condemned.

'Hang on a minute,' some of Paul's readers say. 'That may be true of those pagans bowing before that huge stone statue, but we are God's people. We have the law he gave to Moses after he rescued our ancestors from slavery in Egypt. *We* are not under condemnation.'

Paul sees it differently, for 'it is not the hearers of the law who are righteous before God, but the doers of the law who will be justified' (Romans 2:13). God's people in the Old Testament aren't given a special place because they have his laws. It's those who actually *keep* the law who are 'justified', declared not guilty and in right standing with God. But no one manages to keep the whole law. Even the Jews who were standing and judging the pagan idol worshippers 'practice the very same things' (Romans 2:1).

By the third chapter of the letter Paul reaches the gloomy conclusion that:

> None is righteous, no, not one;
> no one understands;
> no one seeks for God.

Romans 3:10-11

Or, as he puts it a few verses later, 'all have sinned and fall short of the glory of God' (Romans 3:23). God has a standard; there's a mark we need to reach, but none of us do.

That's where we start. We all start condemned. That is our big problem. And that is what the readers of Paul's letter know all too well when he makes the staggering statement, 'There is therefore now *no condemnation* for those who are in Christ Jesus' (Romans 8:1).

No Condemnation

Paul's language here is emphatic; he's shouting it, giving it every stress he can. It's like he's saying, 'Do you get it? Are you really hearing what I'm saying? There's now *no* condemnation.'

But that's not all he says; he also says that there is no condemnation 'for those who are in Christ Jesus'. This is both a condition and an explanation. It's a condition because it puts a limit on those for whom this is true. It's only true of those 'in Christ Jesus'. We've already seen (in *You Are... Chosen*) that to be 'in Christ' is to be united with him so that we receive every spiritual blessing through him. To be 'in Christ' is to be a Christian believer. As we'll soon discover, Paul explains this idea further in Romans 5.

The phrase 'those who are in Christ' is also an explanation of the means by which this freedom from condemnation is achieved. It's the 'how' of the 'what'. For the Christian there is no condemnation because they have been put into Christ's group; it's by being in Christ that we become free from condemnation.

The other amazing thing is that Paul says there is '*now* no condemnation'. This isn't a promise for some far-off time. He isn't reassuring us that when we finally meet God face to face we'll scrape through. He's saying that *right now* there is no condemnation for each and every Christian.

So, if you are a Christian, 'there is therefore now no condemnation'. It's a categorical fact whether you feel it or not, and it's something we need to grasp to really see the extent of what God has done for us and the freedom he has given us.

Therefore

There's one bit of what Paul says that we have yet to consider: the vital word 'therefore'. 'Therefore' tells us that what Paul is saying is a conclusion drawn from what has come before. It's like a huge arrow pointing us to look backwards at what he's already said.

Paul can make the categorical statement that there is 'now no condemnation for those who are in Christ Jesus' because of what he has already said, and so it's vital for us to understand something of what has led him to that point.

Imagine you got into some trouble and ended up owing a huge sum of money to a very dangerous man. One day a random stranger comes up to you in the street. 'Your debts have been paid,' he tells you. 'You can relax now; we're not going to hurt you.' Would you believe him? I'm not sure I would be immediately convinced. I don't think I could just carry on as if there was no longer any threat. I would want to be sure about it somehow. However, if that stranger came to me and explained that my friend had remortgaged his house and paid off the debt with the money, I would find it easier to believe. Understanding *how* it could be true would help me to believe it *was* true.

The same is true when God tells us there is no longer any condemnation for us. If we are going to really believe this, we need to know *how* it's true. Rather than desperately trying to convince ourselves, we need be able to remind ourselves how we *know* it's true.

Adam and Christ

This is what Paul does in Chapter 5. Romans 5:1 is another peak in his argument: 'Therefore, since we have been justified by faith, we have peace with God through our Lord Jesus Christ.' Because Jesus died and took the punishment for our sins we can be justified (made right with God) by putting our faith in him and are therefore at peace with God. Like two enemies reconciled in friendship, we are restored to relationship with God.

The explanation of how we can know there is no condemnation for those 'in Christ Jesus' relies on the idea of humanity being in two distinct groups: those 'in Adam' and those 'in Christ'. Adam, the first man, and Christ are the 'figureheads' of each group. They stand as representatives for their groups, and everyone in each group receives what is due to their representative. Just like those experiences at school where the whole class was punished or excused because of the actions of the one individual, so those 'in Adam' receive what is due to Adam and those 'in Christ' receive what is due to Christ.

Adam And Christ Introduced (Romans 5:12-14)

First Paul starts a comparison that he doesn't actually finish because he realises he needs to clarify things first. 'Just as sin came into the world through one man, and death through sin, and so death spread to all men because all sinned' (v.12). Sin leads to death and so all died because all sinned.

But what does 'all sinned' mean? Well, God didn't give the law to his people until quite a while after Adam. The law was given to Moses and the Israelites after they had been rescued from Egypt (see the Book of Exodus). If there's no law to judge people against, you can't measure sin in the normal way and yet people were still subject to death, the punishment for sin, in the time between Adam and the giving of the law. This means they must have been guilty because of what Adam had done (vv.13-14). The actions of the one affected the many. Just like in the classroom, everyone is considered guilty for the action of that one individual.

In this way, Adam 'was a type of the one who was to come' (v.14). A 'type' is like a picture which foreshadows something. The fact that people are considered guilty because of Adam's sin is a picture which looks forward to how we are considered in relation to Jesus, as we will soon see.

Adam And Christ Contrasted (Romans 5:15-17)

But before he explains the similarity between Adam and Christ, Paul is eager to point out some differences. He doesn't want us to misunderstand what he's saying and have a diminished view of what Jesus has done. Instead he goes to great lengths to show that Jesus is far better than Adam!

First he observes that though many died through Adam's trespass (another word for doing what is wrong before God) 'much more' has the free gift of God come to many. The gift of God's grace is far superior to the result of Adam's sin (v.15).

Verse 16 draws out a second striking contrast. Condemnation came after just one sin but justification (being in the right with God) comes after many trespasses. This highlights how amazing God's love and grace are. Though one sin justly deserves condemnation, God himself provides a solution even after many trespasses.

Finally verse 17 says that though death, as the punishment for sin, 'reigned through that one man' Adam, now *we* are the ones who 'reign in life through...Jesus Christ'. We go from being under the reign of death to reigning in life ourselves.

The two big points here are first that what the one person, Adam or Christ, did affects all those in their groups, and second that being in Christ is far better.

Adam And Christ Compared (Romans 5:18-19)

Finally in verse 18 Paul gets to the point he's been working towards and picks up the train of thought he started and interrupted in verse 12! He now compares Adam and Christ and their representative groups.

> Therefore as one trespass led to condemnation for all men,
> so one act of righteousness leads to justification and life for
> all men.
>
> Romans 5:18

In both, the action of the one individual affects the many. The one trespass of Adam means that all are condemned. But by the same logic, Christ's action offers justification and life to all men. Paul says 'all men' to make the parallel between Adam and Christ clear. He isn't saying that everyone is automatically justified and given new life: the logic doesn't support that. All men are born into Adam, all start off 'in Adam'. Only those who put their faith in Jesus are born again and become 'in Christ'. So all people who are 'in Christ' receive justification and life.

> For as by the one man's disobedience the many were made
> sinners,
> so by the one man's obedience the many will be made
> righteous.
>
> Romans 5:19

Paul makes the same point again in a slightly different way. One man's disobedience can make many sinners (i.e. those who are condemned), so likewise one man's obedience can make many righteous (i.e. not condemned!).

This is how we can *know* that there is 'no condemnation'. If you are a Christian you are 'in Christ' – that is irreversible – you have been taken out of Adam and placed into Christ. And if you are 'in Christ', what is due to Christ is credited to you. Your sins are not and will not be counted against you. If you are in Christ 'there is therefore now no condemnation'.

Do you see that the forgiveness of sins is but the first step, and that the really glorious thing is that we are in Christ, that 'old things are passed away, behold, all things are become new'? We are members of a new race of people ... What grand security we have because we are 'in Christ'! The Christian is not one who is redeemed and saved today but who may fall from it tomorrow and be lost. There is no 'in and out' in salvation. You are either 'in Adam' or you are 'in Christ', and if you are 'in Christ' you have eternal security, you are in Him for ever.

Martyn Lloyd-Jones[a]

Living In The Truth

The statement of Romans 8:1 is categorical – it doesn't depend on how you feel or what you think. It is the truth and we have to choose to live in it. Next time you feel guilty and condemned, remind yourself that you are 'in Christ', and if you are 'in Christ', then everything due to him is given to you. So if you are in Christ 'there is therefore now *no* condemnation'!

---

[a] Martyn Lloyd-Jones, *Romans: An Exposition of Chapter 5: Assurance* (The Banner of Truth Trust, 1971), p.182.

Identity Check-Up

Here are some questions and activities to help you perform an identity check-up.

Understanding Your Identity

Read Romans 5:12-19 and think about these questions.
- What does 'all sinned' (v.12) mean? Is it about something we've done or is there another way in which 'all sinned'?
- In what way was Adam a 'type' (ESV) or 'pattern' (NIV) of Jesus? (v.14)
- What do we get as the result of being 'in Adam'?
- What do we get as the result of being 'in Christ'?
- How can we *know* that we are no longer under condemnation? (Romans 8:1)

Living Your Identity

Take some time to think about these questions or discuss them with others.
- Do you really believe that you are no longer under condemnation? How do you feel when you slip up and sin?
- How can you fight against feeling condemned? What can you build into your life to make sure you enjoy this freedom?
- How does this truth challenge and change the way you think about God and your relationship with him?
- What should be our response to this truth?

3. YOU ARE... FREE FROM CONDEMNATION • 53

Growing In Your Identity

It's easy for us to continue to feel like we're under condemnation even though we are 'in Christ'. We have an enemy who hates seeing people enjoy the reality of what God has done for them. Since he can't do anything to change our identity, all he can do is to try and stop us living in the good of it. Making us feel condemned after we sin is one way he might try to do this.

Think about everything we've said in this chapter and the truths we've found in Paul's letter to the Romans. Complete this quote from Lloyd-Jones with a short paragraph in your own words.[b] What would you say?

> Because this is true of him the Christian should never feel condemnation; he should never allow himself to feel it. The devil will try to make him feel it; but he must answer the devil...

Keep your paragraph somewhere handy. Read it and meditate on it regularly. If you start to feel condemned at some point, grab it and remind yourself how you can *know* that there is no condemnation for those in Christ Jesus.

---

b Quote taken from Martyn Lloyd-Jones, *Romans: An Exposition of Chapters 7.1-8.4 The Law: Its Functions and Limits* (The Banner of Truth Trust, 1973), p.271-272.

CHAPTER 4

You Are... Dead To Sin And Alive To God

¹What shall we say then? Are we to continue in sin that grace may abound? ²By no means! How can we who died to sin still live in it? ³Do you not know that all of us who have been baptized into Christ Jesus were baptized into his death? ⁴We were buried therefore with him by baptism into death, in order that, just as Christ was raised from the dead by the glory of the Father, we too might walk in newness of life.

⁵For if we have been united with him in a death like his, we shall certainly be united with him in a resurrection like his. ⁶We know that our old self was crucified with him in order that the body of sin might be brought to nothing, so that we would no longer be enslaved to sin. ⁷For one who has died has been set free from sin. ⁸Now if we have died with Christ, we believe that we will also live with him. ⁹We know that Christ, being raised from the dead, will never die again; death no longer has dominion over him. ¹⁰For the death he died he died to sin, once for all, but the life

> *he lives he lives to God. ⁱ¹So you also must consider yourselves dead to sin and alive to God in Christ Jesus. ¹²Let not sin therefore reign in your mortal body, to make you obey its passions. ¹³Do not present your members to sin as instruments for unrighteousness, but present yourselves to God as those who have been brought from death to life, and your members to God as instruments for righteousness. ¹⁴For sin will have no dominion over you, since you are not under law but under grace.*
>
> Romans 6:1-14

Understanding True Freedom

There was once a young boy who absolutely loved animals. He loved going to the zoo or the pet shop and dreamed of being a vet when he was older. This boy's grandparents had a small fish tank with one little goldfish. The boy loved watching the little goldfish but he always thought it looked very sad. It didn't move around much, it never responded to him and it didn't even get that excited at feeding time. The boy decided that the tank was just too small for this poor fish and he devised a plan to release it into the wild and give it true freedom.

One day he was at his grandparents'; grandad was out and grandma was in the front garden. He knew this was his chance. He dragged a small chair up to the cabinet where the fish tank sat, plunged his hands in and carefully lifted out the fish. He ran through the house, out the back door all the way to the very end of the garden where he placed the fish on the grass by the hedge before running back and greeting his grandma as if nothing had happened.

Sadly, the fish didn't like his new-found freedom. He didn't feel very free. In fact, he soon didn't feel anything at all. What the little boy didn't realise was that true freedom is the freedom to be what you were made to be. That fish was made to live in water. What seemed to the boy like true freedom was actually, for the fish, a death sentence because it wasn't what he was made for.

Understanding what constitutes true freedom is really important as a Christian. We could hear that we're chosen by God to be new creations who are free from condemnation and think, 'Great, so now I can do what I like. In fact, if I sin it just makes God's free gift of forgiveness look even more amazing, right?' But that would be a misunderstanding of true freedom. The truth is, we were made for something better than a life of sin, and we'll only find true freedom when we live in line with that plan.

It seems that Paul knew that some people might respond to his teaching this way, misunderstanding what true freedom is, and so in Romans 6 he explains that actually, the true freedom of a Christian is the freedom to not sin.

Dying With Christ And Dying To Sin

'What shall we say then? Are we to continue in sin so that grace may abound?' (Romans 6:1). Paul knows that this is the sort of thing some people might say when they realise they are free from condemnation so he makes it clear that such ideas are a complete misunderstanding of what it means to be a Christian.

Christians are 'in Christ'; we are united with Jesus so that in some way we have gone through what he went through. Paul says that when we were baptised into Christ we were 'baptised into his death' (Romans 6:3). Baptism is a picture of being united with Christ. He's not saying that by being baptised we become united with Christ but that baptism is an acting out of what has already happened. So baptism is a visible representation of the fact that as Christians we have died with Christ when he died on the cross.

When we died with Christ 'our old self was crucified with him... so that we would no longer be enslaved to sin' (Romans 6:6). Before becoming Christians and being united with Christ we were slaves of sin. Sin was an unstoppable force which had power over us. Because we were 'in Adam' we were born with an inbuilt urge to sin. When we were children we didn't need to be taught how to be bad; it came naturally to us all. When we're 'in Adam' being bad comes to us more naturally than being good (Ephesians 2:1-3; Psalm 51:5). But now, that old self has been crucified with Jesus on the cross and the power sin had over us is broken. We are left free to not sin.

But it doesn't stop there because Jesus didn't just die; he also rose from the dead, and because he rose from the dead, he will never die again. Now 'the life he lives he lives to God' (Romans 6:10). If we are united with him then we also live a new life. Paul doesn't actually say that we are raised with Christ because that is something we are still waiting for, the day when Jesus returns bringing the new creation and when we will be raised with new bodies just as he was. But something of the power of Jesus' resurrection is given to us now so that we can 'walk in newness of life' (Romans 6:4). This life is a life where we are no longer under the power of sin but are free to live our lives to God and experience true freedom: the freedom not to sin but to live righteous lives.

Consider Yourselves...

Paul tells us to 'count' (NIV), 'consider' (ESV) or 'reckon' (KJV) ourselves as 'dead to sin and alive to God in Christ Jesus' (Romans

6:11). This isn't about trying really hard to convince ourselves something is true even though we actually know it isn't. It's about teaching ourselves and reminding ourselves that this is already true. In the film *The Bourne Identity*, Jason Bourne, a CIA agent, is lifted out of the sea by some fishermen after being thrown into the sea in a failed mission. Bourne has been seriously injured and has lost all memory of who he is. As the film goes on he discovers more and more about his true identity and about his life, and even though his memory doesn't return and he doesn't necessarily feel like the person he discovers he was before the accident, he knows it's true and so he has to reckon it so. He has to choose to believe who he actually is. In the same way we have to reckon it as true that we have died to sin, because we have.

If you are a Christian, you have been united with Christ in his death and so you have died to sin and are now alive to God. Reckon it so!

The original response to Paul's teaching given in Romans 6:1 interpreted grace as a reason to sin. Having shown that that completely misunderstands what God has done for Christians, Paul inverts that understanding of grace. Grace doesn't lead us to sin but rather 'sin will have no dominion over you, since you are not under law but under grace' (Romans 6:14). When we're under God's grace we have been set free from the power of sin. We are brought into true freedom, the freedom to not sin.

Freedom In Slavery

In the second half of Romans 6, Paul responds to another question, very similar to that posed in verse 1. In this response he goes on to expand what he's already told us to show that actually the freedom we get by being united with Christ in his death isn't the freedom to be our own people but the freedom to be slaves 'of obedience' (Romans 6:16), 'slaves of righteousness' (Romans 6:18) and 'slaves of God' (Romans 6:22).

It turns out there is no such thing as a free person. You're either a slave to sin or a slave to obedience. So we have been set free from sin and have become slaves of righteousness (Romans 6:18).

Slaves are under the control of their masters. What the master says goes. The master of a slave has power over them. We've seen that when we were slaves of sin it had this sort of power over us. We naturally tended towards sin, and without some sort of external help we were trapped in a life of sinful actions.

But if we're now slaves of righteousness then the power over us is completely different. We haven't just been freed from the power of sin; we've been brought into a new situation where we are given the power to live righteous lives, as God wants us to and as he originally created us to. Being a slave to righteousness means that God is giving us power to live the way he wants us to. Elsewhere in the New Testament this power is explained as the power of the Holy Spirit, who comes and lives inside of us to help us live holy lives (Romans 7:6; Galatians 5:16-24).

Knowing This Freedom

So the way we battle sin is to recognise who we already are and step into that truth. How might that work in reality?

First, we need to know the truth. Hopefully this chapter has helped you start to get a grasp of it. There are also lots of other sections of the New Testament which can help us understand this truth. Take a look at some of them and let the truth they contain root itself deeply in you (e.g. Galatians 5:13-26; Ephesians 4:17-5:21; 1 Peter 1:13-2:12).

Second, we need to be constantly reminding ourselves of this truth. Day in, day out, we need to remind ourselves of our identity. The world and the devil will try to tell us lies and rob us of these truths; we need to fight to keep hold of them. This is also important because if we can get them firmly within our thinking when we're not facing significant temptation, we'll find it much easier to apply them when we are.

Third, when those moments of temptation come we need to battle by reminding ourselves of the truth; that's the time to reckon ourselves dead to sin but alive to God. If we're doing this regularly it will be much easier to do at these times. When you're tempted, remind yourself that you no longer have to do this stuff, that you were once enslaved to these ideas and desires but they died with Christ. Remind yourself that you are now a slave of righteousness, free not to sin, with the power of the Holy Spirit helping you choose the better way. Pray, cry out to God that he would come and strengthen you to live out your new identity with the help of his Holy Spirit. Then 'sin will have no dominion over you, since you are not under law but under grace' (Romans 6:14).

Identity Check-Up

Here are some questions and activities to help you perform an identity check-up.

Understanding Your Identity

Read Romans 6:1-23 and think about these questions.
- What was our situation in relation to sin before we became Christians? (vv.6, 17, 20-21)
- How does this situation change when we become Christians? (vv.4, 11, 18, 22)
- What does the idea of slavery say about the nature of these relationships?
- How does baptism form a useful illustration of the truth Paul talks about in Romans 6?

Living Your Identity

Take some time to think about these questions or discuss them with others.
- 'If there's no condemnation for me because I'm "in Christ" I can keep doing what I like. It makes no difference.' How would you respond to a friend who said this to you?
- What can we do to get this truth deeply embedded in us and how can we use it to fight temptation?
- How should the combination of this chapter and the previous chapter (*You Are... Free from Condemnation*) shape the way we respond to and seek to help a Christian who comes to us and confesses they are struggling with repeated sin?

Growing In Your Identity

'No temptation has overtaken you that is not common to man. God is faithful, and he will not let you be tempted beyond your ability, but with the temptation he will also provide the way of escape, that you may be able to endure it' (1 Corinthians 10:13).

We will all face temptation. But God has promised us that he will never let that temptation be too strong for us to resist and he will always offer us a way to escape from it. We've seen in this chapter that we need to grow in our appreciation of the truth that we have died to sin and are now enslaved to God.

Write a paragraph which summarises this truth for yourself. You might want to do it in the form of a poem or a short song. Stick in on your fridge or the bathroom mirror or somewhere where you will see it regularly. Every time you see it, stop, read it and thank God for the truth it contains.

When you feel tempted, use this paragraph to help you battle.

CHAPTER 5

You Are... Dead To The Law

^{1}Or do you not know, brothers—for I am speaking to those who know the law—that the law is binding on a person only as long as he lives? ^{2}For a married woman is bound by law to her husband while he lives, but if her husband dies she is released from the law of marriage. ^{3}Accordingly, she will be called an adulteress if she lives with another man while her husband is alive. But if her husband dies, she is free from that law, and if she marries another man she is not an adulteress.

^{4}Likewise, my brothers, you also have died to the law through the body of Christ, so that you may belong to another, to him who has been raised from the dead, in order that we may bear fruit for God. ^{5}For while we were living in the flesh, our sinful passions, aroused by the law, were at work in our members to bear fruit for death. ^{6}But now we are released from the law, having died to that *which held us captive, so that we serve in the new way of the Spirit and not in the old way of the written code*

Romans 7:1-6

Dead Men Being Executed?

The 30th January 1661 is one of the weirdest days in British history. On that day, in London, four dead men were executed. These men had been key players in the overthrow of the monarchy in Britain. However, when the monarchy was re-established by the son of the king whom Oliver Cromwell and these men had executed, they were found guilty of high treason; their bodies were dug up, hanged and beheaded.

It's not very often that a dead person receives a punishment on earth for a crime. That's because laws are for the living. While we live in a certain place or under a certain ruler, we are bound by their laws and can be found guilty and punished if we fail to keep them. But when we die the power exercised over us by those laws is broken. Laws are for the living.

This is important for us as Christians. The Bible is full of laws; the first five books are sometimes just called 'The Law'. The place of the Old Testament law in the life of Christians is a tricky question, one which confuses and worries many people. Are we still meant to keep the law? We know we're meant to be living holy lives, trying to do what's right and not do what's wrong. But then we know we're saved by grace not by works of the law, so perhaps we don't have to follow the law. It doesn't take long before our heads are spinning and we don't know what to think.

Well thankfully Paul knew that this is a tricky subject for Christians and so he dedicates several paragraphs to explaining it in Romans. Some of us might find that what he says is quite a surprise.

Laws For The Living

Despite the fact that history is peppered with the occasional odd story suggesting something different (such as the British revolutionaries mentioned above) most people, in most cultures, would agree that 'the law is binding on a person only as long as he lives' (Romans 7:1). I'm a citizen of the United Kingdom and so am under the laws of the United Kingdom. However, when I die they will no longer have any say over me. Death brings release from the law. Laws are for the living.

Paul applies this idea to God's law, given to Israel at Mount Sinai and recorded in the Old Testament, and illustrates it by using one particular law – the law of marriage (Romans 7:2-3). When a man and woman marry they are joined together under law for life. If one of them goes off and starts a relationship with someone else while the other is still alive, they're committing adultery. But the important point is that if one of the pair dies, the other is free to marry someone else and won't be committing adultery. Why? Because death breaks the power of law. The law of marriage shows us the general principle that laws are for the living.

Dying To The Law

As Christians our relationship to the Old Testament law relies on this principle. Before we become Christians our relationship to the law is like being married to the worst husband in the world. This husband spends all his time telling us what we should do, telling us what we shouldn't do and pointing out when we get it wrong, all while he is doing absolutely nothing to help. He's constantly nagging and criticising while he just sits around doing nothing. To make it even worse, this husband will never die. Jesus told us that the law will never pass away (Matthew 5:18). We're trapped under the law.

But as we've seen (*You Are... Dead to Sin*), we have died with Christ by being united with him in his death (Romans 6:3-4). So whereas the law will never die, we have died through the death of Jesus. If we've died then the law has no hold over us any more. Laws are for the living. 'But now we are released from the law, having died to that which held us captive' (Romans 7:6). The law no longer has any power over us. It has no claim on our allegiance and no right to condemn us.

As Terry Virgo puts it, we're like a soldier who has been discharged. As we go to leave the barracks a sergeant major might see us and command us to straighten up and return to our post. But we've been discharged, the sergeant major no longer has any power over us. 'Let the sergeant-major become ever so red in the face, let the veins stand out ever so prominently on his neck, it's of no consequence. He cannot command the discharged soldier any more!'[a]

The law has no right to accuse us since we have died to it and God has declared that there is 'no condemnation for those who are in Christ Jesus' (Romans 8:1 – *You Are... Free From Condemnation*). Sometimes we might still feel condemned, like we're not doing well enough, but that's the time when we need to remind ourselves of the truth. The law has no right to make us feel condemned. When it does, we're believing a lie.

---

[a] Terry Virgo, *The Spirit-Filled Church* (Monarch Books, 2011), pp.58-59.

A New Way To Live

But that's not all Paul says when he's discussing the place of the law in our lives. He doesn't leave it there as if we're now left with no help and no guidance as to how to live. God has done something even better than just releasing us from the power of the law: he's given us a new way to live, a new power by which to live holy lives. Paul tells us that we have been released from the law 'so that we serve in the new way of the Spirit and not in the old way of the written code' (Romans 7:6).

The law can never give us the power to live a holy life. In fact, the law aroused our sinful passions so that we ended up sinning more (Romans 7:5). The law has the opposite effect to what we might expect. It's like when you tell a child (or an adult!) not to do something and all they then want to do is that exact thing. The law will never empower us to live a life more in line with what God wants and what we were made for. Neither will making more rules and regulations for ourselves. Making a rule that we're going to get up an hour earlier to pray and read the Bible or that we're not going to watch those sex-fuelled adverts will never, on their own, help us change.

But there is good news. The Spirit of God can help us change. We are now new creations (2 Corinthians 5:17 – *You Are... A New Creation*) inside whom God lives by his Spirit, and his Spirit living in us finally gives us the power to live a holy life. Paul expresses this in different words when he says that we have died to the law so that we can 'belong to another, to him who has been raised from the dead, in order that we may bear fruit for God' (Romans 7:4). Fruit is something that grows naturally. Trees don't strive to produce fruit; they do it naturally because of what they are. So too for us the fruit of living God's way grows naturally out of who he has made us to be, not through our striving.

When we're fighting temptation, we need to ask the Holy Spirit to help us. The same point is made clear when Paul writes to the Galatians, 'Walk by the Spirit, and you will not gratify the desires of the flesh ... If you are led by the Spirit, you are not under the law' (Galatians 5:16, 18). God's plan in saving us has always been that we would return to holy living. Salvation isn't just a ticket to heaven. When Paul opens his letter to the Romans he talks about his call from God to be an apostle but he doesn't say the purpose was to save people from hell or that people might be forgiven for their sins. Rather he says it was 'to bring about the obedience of faith for the sake of his name among all the nations' (Romans 1:5). The end goal of salvation is becoming the holy people God made us to be, living in relationship with him, all of which is ultimately so that God would be worshipped ('for the sake of his name').

Walking In Freedom

Our freedom from the law, like so many of the elements of our identity we're exploring, is a categorical fact about our present state. It's something that really has already happened to us. But that doesn't guarantee we'll be experiencing the freedom it offers us. Experiencing that freedom is a choice we have to make.

It seems that when Paul wrote to the church in Galatia, some people there weren't living in the light of their freedom from the law and were teaching that it was necessary to keep the law to be in God's people. But Paul responds clearly: 'For freedom Christ has set us free; stand firm therefore, and do not submit again to a yoke of slavery' (Galatians 5:1). It's a past tense fact that Christ has set us free from the law, but sometimes we put ourselves back under the law by trying to use it to live a holy life. It's like returning to an old slave master who still won't do anything to help us. It's madness. We need to remember that we live 'in the new way of the Spirit and not in the old way of the written code' (Romans 7:6).

The law might offer us some sort of insight into God's moral will, into what is right and what is wrong. But if we try to live by it and legislate for ourselves and others we're just returning to a fruitless slavery. Instead we need to be filled with the Spirit and ask God to empower us more and more to live holy lives each and every day.

Identity Check-Up

Here are some questions and activities to help you perform an identity check-up.

Understanding Your Identity

Read Romans 7:1-6 and think about these questions.
- In what way is our relationship to the law, now that we are 'in Christ', parallel to being freed from a bad marriage? (vv.1-4)
- What is the purpose of us dying to the law? (vv.4-6)
- What is the significance of the imagery of bearing fruit when compared to trying to keep a law? (v.4)
- What is different about how we live now that we have died to the law? (v.6)

Living Your Identity

Take some time to think about these questions or discuss them with others.

- What have you done or used in the past to try and help you live God's way? Did these things work?
- Are there any laws you have been living under (either because you put them there yourself or someone else forced them upon you) which have been making you feel condemned and stealing the freedom God has given you?
- What can we do to help ourselves live God's way? How should this play out in our lives each day?

Growing In Your Identity

Paul says that the new freedom we have to live God's way is like the life in a plant that bears fruit. Fruit trees and bushes naturally and easily produce fruit when they are in the right conditions. However, if they aren't given those good conditions, or if weeds or other things get in the way, they won't produce fruit.

The same is true for us. To bear good fruit we need to create the right conditions in our lives and get rid of anything that gets in the way.

Doing Some Weeding

Sometimes we are hindered from bearing fruit by rules and laws we are living under. These might be things we have put in place ourselves or that others have imposed on us. In themselves they might not be bad things. Wanting to pray more or to stop lying are great goals but they become damaging when we set them up as rules, which we then fail to keep and so they leave us feeling condemned. God has freed us from condemnation and the law so that we no longer have to experience that sense of guilt.

Ask God to reveal to you any rules you are living under which have actually been preventing you from bearing fruit and have been leaving you feeling guilty. You may well be so used to these that you don't even realise they're there. Allow time for God to speak to you and to highlight things to you. When he does, declare that you have died to that rule or law and ask him to help you to be free from it.

Doing Some Watering

Paul says that we now 'serve in the new way of the Spirit' (Romans 7:6). God's Holy Spirit living in us is the vital water we need to bear fruit for God.

Spend some time asking God to fill you with his Holy Spirit. If there are particular areas of life or of your character that you know aren't in line with the way God made you to be, ask him to come and help you in those areas by his Spirit.

We need to ask God to fill us with his Spirit to help us live his way every day, and need to do a check as often as possible for those weeds which creep in and condemn us.

CHAPTER 6

You Are... Adopted

> ^{14}*For all who are led by the Spirit of God are sons of God. ^{15}For you did not receive the spirit of slavery to fall back into fear, but you have received the Spirit of adoption as sons, by whom we cry, 'Abba! Father.' ^{16}The Spirit himself bears witness with our spirit that we are children of God, ^{17}and if children, then heirs—heirs of God and fellow heirs with Christ, provided we suffer with him in order that we may also be glorified with him.*
> Romans 8:14-17

'I've Adopted A...'

These days you can adopt just about anything. If you type 'Adopt a' into Google the suggestions it gives include a sloth, a penguin, a snow leopard, a donkey and a tiger. You can even adopt an acre of rainforest, grassland or coral reef. When you sign up for one of these programmes you get a certificate and a picture, maybe even a soft toy, but there's something missing: what you don't get is relationship. Even if you adopt a sloth and travel to South America and track down your sloth, it probably won't be particularly interested in meeting you.

Lack of relationship also means there's a lack of security. This sort of adoption isn't for life: as soon as money gets a bit tight you can just cancel the adoption and stop paying for your animal or place. Real adoption isn't like that. Real adoption is about relationship and security.

A Good Deal

The previous chapters have focussed on things which are mostly what we might call legal. They are about where we stand in relation to God, sin and the law. But adoption is about relationship. There's an important legal basis to our adoption, but that's only half the story.

Imagine you'd fallen on hard times and had got into drink or drugs. You ended up involved in a gang who committed a violent crime to fund their addictions. It's your time to appear in court and the evidence is pretty damning. But to your amazement the verdict which comes back is that you're 'not guilty'. There's no condemnation – someone else has taken that for you. That's a pretty good deal. But then the judge starts talking to you and tells you that he's going to help you. He's going to organise support so you can quit the drink and the drugs and stay away from the people who led you astray. Those things that had had power over you, which you felt unable to resist but which were ruining your life, are dealt with. You've got a chance to start afresh. That's an even better deal. But then the judge starts to get down from his seat and walks towards you. You start wondering what he's going to do. Was this just a cruel joke? Is he about to send you to prison after all? He walks right up to you, puts his arm around you and says, 'And now I'm going to adopt you, I'm going to walk through this with you, support you and one day you'll inherit my estate'. Now that, is a good deal!

That's what God has done for us. Adoption didn't have to be part of God's plan of salvation. He owed us nothing and yet not only does he forgive us, he also makes us his children and heirs. No wonder John proclaimed, 'See what great love the Father has lavished on us, that we should be called children of God! And that is what we are!' (1 John 3:1 NIV).

The Spirit Of Adoption As Sons

Adoption is another key element of our identity which Paul discusses in his letter to the Christians in Rome. In Romans 8, after he's looked at the blessings of being 'in Christ' which we discussed in the previous chapters, he talks about the Christian life, a life lived 'in the Spirit', and the Christian hope for the future.

Having just explained that as Christians we no longer live controlled by the flesh but by the Spirit (as we saw in *You Are... Dead to Sin*), he then tells us that 'all who are led by the Spirit of God are sons of God' (Romans 8:14). By this he means that all Christians are already sons of God since Paul is clear in Romans 8 that the Holy Spirit is at work in all Christians (Romans 8:9). This doesn't refer to some special, ultra-holy group of Christians but to all of us.

That Paul says we are 'sons' not 'sons and daughters' is important. In the ancient world in which Paul lived it was the eldest son who gained the inheritance from the father, even if he had older sisters. As we shall see, inheritance is a big part of our adoption. We see that Paul includes both men and women as 'sons' in verse 16 where he uses the general term 'children of God'.

Christian men have to cope with being the bride of Christ (Ephesians 5:25-33); Christian women have to cope with being sons. Both are good things!

The following verse explains how this happens. We have received a Spirit of adoption, who it becomes apparent is the Holy Spirit (Romans 8:15). Adoption now and in the ancient world is about a legal move from one family to another. As an adopted child you become a full member of your new family and an heir. When Paul was writing, having an heir was vital. Society was all about families and their honour and so it was important to have an heir to continue the family line. If a couple who were Roman citizens didn't manage to have a child naturally they would adopt a son, often the child of a slave. The child would be chosen and redeemed (i.e. bought out of slavery) and enter the new family. Even though the child came from a slave family and so had little in the way of rights or hope for the future, when he was legally adopted he was considered a full member of the new family and would become the Roman man's heir. The adopted son would be no different in terms of rights to a son the couple might have had naturally. So when Paul says we have 'received the Spirit of adoption' he means that we have been legally made sons of God, with all the current privileges of a son, and the future hope of one who will inherit.

Living As Sons

These verses also tell us something about the difference our adoption makes to our lives. First, the Spirit we have received is not 'the spirit of slavery' (Romans 8:15). Before we were 'in Christ' and were adopted, we were enslaved to sin and to the law, as we've seen in the previous chapters. Like many of the boys adopted in the ancient world, we too were slaves. We've come from a position where we had nothing and no hope, a position of fear, to one where we no longer need 'to fall back into fear'. We are no longer slaves but sons. So we no longer need to live in fear of the condemnation of God because we are free from condemnation. We no longer need to live in the fear of the power of sin or the accusations of the law because we have been bought out of that slavery. In fact, we no longer need fear anything because we are secure in God's family.

The second difference receiving the Spirit of adoption makes is that he helps us to really know and believe who we are 'in Christ'. By this Spirit we cry out, '*Abba!* Father!' (Romans 8:15). *Abba* is an Aramaic word (one of the languages spoken by the Jewish people in Jesus' day) which means 'daddy'. But unlike our English word 'daddy', which tends mostly to be used by young children, it's a word that was used by grown-up children too. It speaks of deep relationship and intimacy. Jesus used the word *abba* when he prayed to God (e.g. Mark 14:36) and his disciples clearly felt that this was something quite special since they preserved it in the gospels, and Paul uses it twice in his letters (Romans 8:15; Galatians 4:6). So this Spirit of adoption does something in our spirits which makes us cry out with this expression of intimacy and affection. As verse 16 explains it, 'the Spirit himself bears witness with our spirit that we are children of God'. The Holy Spirit speaks to our own spirits and makes this truth hit home. If we struggle to believe that we are God's sons we need to invite God's Spirit to come and work in our own spirits to help us experience the reality of this truth.

But there's still one more thing. If we are God's children then we are also heirs, 'heirs of God and fellow heirs with Christ'

(Romans 8:17). Not only does being adopted by God give us a genuine experience of an intimate relationship with him, which frees us from all fear; we are also made his heirs. We will inherit from God. What do we inherit? The rest of Romans 8 covers that question. We inherit the fulfilment of God's promises made to his people in the Old Testament. Inheritance is a big theme in the Old Testament as its whole story (and indeed the story of the whole Bible) is about God fulfilling his promises to restore and repair everything that was lost and broken when Adam and Eve sinned in the Garden of Eden (Genesis 2-3). Our inheritance is resurrection to new life in God's perfect new creation (Romans 8:20-25). God is going to take away all the pain and all the hurt. All the damage of sin to relationships and to the physical world will be done away with and all those 'in Christ' will be raised to eternal life with him in a perfect new creation. That is the awesome inheritance we get as the sons of God.

But Paul doesn't even stop there. Perhaps to our surprise he adds another phrase: 'provided we suffer with him in order that we may also be glorified with him' (Romans 8:17). Jesus won his victory through suffering. He suffered, humbling himself to death, and was then glorified (Philippians 2:6-11). This is the pattern of God's kingdom. God's people, in this world, will be sufferers. It's a natural consequence of being a Christian.

But it's suffering which is endured through the strengthening of God's Spirit and the sure hope of our inheritance as sons. And just as Jesus suffered and was glorified, so we also suffer but will then be glorified to receive this inheritance.

Experiencing Sonship

Several key points come out of Paul's discussion of adoption here and in a similar passage when he writes to the churches in Galatia (Galatians 4:1-6). It's worth summarising how they should make an impact in our lives.

Adoption is a now/not-yet experience. That means that even though Jesus has won the decisive victory over sin, death and evil through his death and resurrection, we are still waiting to see some of the fruits of that victory. Some of them we experience now, in this life: they're the 'now' elements. But others we are not yet experiencing: they're the 'not-yet' elements. It's as if Jesus wrote and signed a whole load of cheques when he died on the cross and rose back to life. These cheques are imperishable; nothing can destroy them. Some have already been taken to the bank and cashed in but there are others which God, in his wisdom, is still holding, waiting to cash them in when Jesus returns. Like many parts of the Christian life, adoption sits in this tension. There are aspects of our adoption that we experience now and others that we are still waiting for.

Adoption In The Now...

The Bible is clear that all Christians are adopted as God's sons now. The legal exchange has happened. God has redeemed us out of our slavery and made us his own children. This means there is awesome *security* for God's children. We are members of the family now. We are loved, safe and secure. We're not house guests who are allowed to stay as long as we behave ourselves. We are legally bound to our new father. If you want to see what this father is like and how he feels about us when we rebel against him, take a look at the parable of the Prodigal Son (Luke 15:11-32).

If we're secure we are also *safe*. Our new position is an invitation to live without fear. Our new father has accepted us fully and will forever be a perfect father. We need not be afraid of him or anyone or anything else.

The Spirit of adoption gives us a genuine experience of deep *intimacy* with God. God isn't a distant or stern father; he is a loving, perfect father. No matter what our experience of earthly fathers, God offers perfect fathering. The Holy Spirit can make this truth real to us. We need to ask him and invite him to do that. For Paul, security wasn't experienced either through knowing the truth or through experiencing the witness of the Holy Spirit, but through both together. We need both too. When the Spirit works in us he will produce in us that cry of intimacy: '*Abba!* Father!'

A wise friend once said to me, 'The only thing you can guarantee as a parent is that you'll get it wrong.' To a greater or lesser extent all of us will have a distorted picture of what a good father is because of our earthly experiences. God is the only perfect father and we need to let him reveal to us what he's really like.

Sometimes if we've had particularly bad experiences of fathering on earth, this truth can be hard for us to believe and enjoy. There are three things which can help in these situations. First is a genuine hunger to experience God's fathering love, expressed in heartfelt prayer that the Holy Spirit would bear witness to our own spirit that we are a son of God. Second is a deep appreciation of the truth of who we are 'in Christ'. Not just the biblical truth about our adoption but about all the elements of our identity, so we begin to see ourselves as our heavenly father does. Biblical truth about who we are 'in Christ' isn't just words or knowledge; it's the wisdom of God, powerful realities about what

God has done in history and in our lives. As we constantly pour these truths into our hearts God will take what we know and make it real to us through the Holy Spirit. Both the Spirit and truth are needed. They are not opposed but work together. Finally, God can use other people to mediate love to us and heal the wounds which our experiences may have left. If an individual has a bad experience of fathering or mothering as they grow up, this can have a deep effect on how they develop emotionally. God made us to be in relationship with others, and a loving family home is a vital part of our early development. When this goes wrong (and we need to not be afraid to admit that it often does: we live in a fallen world where there is no perfect parenting), God can use other people to help meet some of those needs and heal the wounds. This doesn't stand in opposition to letting God bring healing; much like using medicine for a physical illness, it can be one of many ways God works for our good.

Intimacy allows *communication.* Adoption is an invitation and assertion of the right to be in constant communication with God. Just as Jesus prayed, '*Abba,* Father' (Mark 14:36), we too can build our relationship with our new father through honest and open communication. God wants us to talk with him and longs for us to hear him when he responds.

Adoption In The Not-Yet...

But there are also elements of our adoption which are still to come. Paul talks of the 'redemption of our bodies' as part of our adoption which we are still eagerly waiting for (Romans 8:23). That will come on the day when we are raised with new, incorruptible bodies.

Our inheritance is another 'not-yet' element. We still wait for that perfect new creation and the eternal life we will enjoy with God there. Suffering will inevitably come before we reach that point, but the guarantee of our inheritance is a support and motivation to us in those times.

Identity Check-Up

Here are some questions and activities to help you perform an identity check-up.

Understanding Your Identity

Read Romans 8:12-17 and think about these questions.
- What are the three things that the Spirit of adoption does for us? (vv.15-16)
- Why is it significant that we are adopted as 'sons' (rather than sons and daughters)?
- What does it mean to be an heir of God and fellow heir of Christ? You might want to read on in Romans 8.
- How does suffering relate to our adoption? (v.17)

Living Your Identity

Take some time to think about these questions or discuss them with others.
- What images and associations does the idea of God as father create in your mind?
- To what extent does your position as a son who has received the Spirit of adoption affect your life at the moment? Is this an aspect of your identity you regularly think about?

- How should being adopted by God affect our lives?
- What does or could get in the way of living in your position as a son and heir? What do you need to do to more actively live out your position as a son and heir of God?

Growing In Your Identity

Most of us will have a skewed picture of what a father is like. God is the only perfect father, and for all of us our earthly experiences will have shaped the way see God as father.

- Take some time to think about the idea of a father. Write down the things associated with fathers in your mind. Don't try and come up with the right answers; just put down what is true for you.
- Take some time to read the parable of the Prodigal Son (Luke 15:11-32), thinking at each stage about the actions and attitudes of the father.
- Divide a piece of paper in half, one side headed 'Imperfect Fathers', the other 'The Perfect Father'. Go back to the ideas you wrote down earlier and put them in the relevant column. Add to The Perfect Father column anything else you learnt about God the father from the parable or from our look at Romans 8.
- Spend some time praying that God would take away the associations you have in The Imperfect Fathers column and that the Holy Spirit would help you to encounter God as the perfect father.
- You may find that you need to forgive your earthly family. Forgiving is choosing not to hold something against someone, even when it's still painful, and letting God deal with the other person. It's often hard to really encounter God

as father while we still hold unforgiveness towards earthly families in our hearts. You might want to talk and pray with a church leader or trusted Christian friend about this.

CHAPTER 7

You Are... A Witness

⁴⁴Then he said to them, "These are my words that I spoke to you while I was still with you, that everything written about me in the Law of Moses and the Prophets and the Psalms must be fulfilled." ⁴⁵Then he opened their minds to understand the Scriptures, ⁴⁶and said to them, "Thus it is written, that the Christ should suffer and on the third day rise from the dead, ⁴⁷and that repentance and forgiveness of sins should be proclaimed in his name to all nations, beginning from Jerusalem. ⁴⁸You are witnesses of these things. ⁴⁹And behold, I am sending the promise of my Father upon you. But stay in the city until you are clothed with power from on high."

Luke 24:44-49

⁶So when they had come together, they asked him, "Lord, will you at this time restore the kingdom to Israel?" ⁷He said to them, "It is not for you to know times or seasons that the Father has fixed by his own authority. ⁸But you will receive power when the Holy Spirit has come upon you, and you will be my witnesses in

Jerusalem and in all Judea and Samaria, and to the end of the earth." [9] And when he had said these things, as they were looking on, he was lifted up, and a cloud took him out of their sight. [10] And while they were gazing into heaven as he went, behold, two men stood by them in white robes, [11] and said, "Men of Galilee, why do you stand looking into heaven? This Jesus, who was taken up from you into heaven, will come in the same way as you saw him go into heaven."

Acts 1:6-11

Christian Lingo

Do you remember when you first became a Christian and started mixing with other Christians? Did you find yourself a bit confused by all the lingo people were throwing around as if it should be obvious what they were talking about? *Quiet time*, *worldly*, *fellowship*, *pressing in*, *naturally supernatural*, *emergent*, *godhead*... All of these are Christian lingo. For better or worse, part of getting used to your new life as a Christian is working out what people are on about half of the time. (Perhaps this is something we should all think about, but that's for another time!)

Witnessing is another of those words. Outside of the Christian world, to be a witness means to report to others what you saw or experienced at a certain time or place. The most obvious example is when people are witnesses in a legal trial: they stand up in court and report to those present what they saw or what they know about the defendant. However, in the world of Christian lingo, witnessing has been hijacked and evokes ideas of door knocking and little booklets, along with feelings of fear, pressure and guilt. I often wonder what Jesus would think of our modern-day Christian lingo. In the case of witnessing, I think he would warn us we've made our own meaning for the word. When he talked about being his witnesses, it was a lot easier than we tend to make it.

Being A Witness, Ready To Witness

Luke wrote two books which are in the New Testament that were designed to be a two-part work and, oddly, in our modern Bibles are separated from each other by the Gospel of John. The two volumes of Luke's work (Luke's Gospel and the Acts of the Apostles) are closely tied together by lots of things, including the theme of witnessing.

At the end of his account of Jesus' life (Luke 24:44-49) Luke tells us that the risen Jesus appeared to the disciples and said to them, 'You are witnesses of these things' (Luke 24:48). Here 'witnesses' is something they already are. They are people who have witnessed, seen and experienced these things. What are 'these things'? It must be what Jesus has just explained to them – the truth that he, as the long-awaited Christ, was killed but rose again after three days so that 'repentance and forgiveness of sins should be proclaimed in his name to all nations' (Luke 24:47). They had seen Jesus die and seen him after he had risen from the dead, and he had opened their minds to understand what had happened and how it fitted into God's big plan to save the world (Luke 24:44-45).

In the first chapter of Luke's second volume (Acts 1:6-11) Jesus tells the disciples, 'You will be my witnesses' (Acts 1:8). Here the focus is different. Having been witnesses by observing the events of Jesus' life and death, they will now become witnesses in a different sense by going on to report to others what they have seen and experienced. The two passages talk about two steps in the process of witnessing. First they saw, experienced and understood the event and then they went on to report it to others.

Are We Really Witnesses?

Our situation is a little different, but not totally so. We may not have seen Jesus in the flesh as the disciples had but as Christians we have experienced and witnessed what he does. We are witnesses of the truth and power of the Gospel because as Christians we have believed in it and received its blessings. We are witnesses of the fact that Jesus has risen from the dead and is alive. We are witnesses to the fact that God offers salvation to all who put their faith in him. We are witnesses to the fact that God grants fullness of life to those who believe in Jesus.

Part of the witness of these first Christians was also to write the gospels or to pass their memories of what they had witnessed with Jesus on to others to record for us. We also become witnesses of Jesus when we read the gospels and see what he was like, what he did and what he taught.

Just as we are witnesses from our own experience, we are also called to be witnesses, to report this understanding and experience to others. Being a witness is very simple really. If I was called up to be a witness of a crime I had seen, it wouldn't be too much hard work for me. I saw the event so all I need to do is report what I saw and answer any questions I'm asked. Being a witness for Jesus is the same. It's not about door knocking, giving out leaflets or shouting on a street corner (though done rightly all of these can be ways of witnessing); it's just telling others what we've found to be true about God.

When we get out of the Christian lingo understanding of witnessing it becomes a lot easier and a lot less scary. It's something we can naturally do with our friends and family and those we come into contact with in daily life. And that's not all: Jesus doesn't stop there; he promises something else too.

You Will Receive Power

On both occasions when Jesus talks to the disciples about being witnesses he promises to send them the Holy Spirit who will give them power (Luke 24:49; Acts 1:8). The Holy Spirit is intimately connected with being a witness for God. He's the third person of the Trinity. (More Christian lingo! That means that just like God the Father and Jesus, he is fully God while also being a separate figure from God the Father and Jesus. God is three persons in one. Impossible? God doesn't seem to think so.) The Holy Spirit has lots of roles in the life of a Christian; we've already seen that he helps us know that we have been adopted by God and we'll soon see that he gives us all gifts to enable us to do his work. But one of the most important roles of the Holy Spirit according to the New Testament is to empower us to be witnesses for God.

We see this with the disciples. Here are a few average men who have been called by Jesus to follow him and learn from him. Perhaps not surprisingly, when Jesus is arrested by the Romans they flee, terrified of what might happen to them if they are associated with him. This doesn't even seem to have changed much once Jesus had risen from the dead. John tells us that the disciples kept themselves in a locked room out of fear of the Jewish leaders, even after they had found the empty tomb and after Mary Magdalene had met the risen Jesus. In fact, even a week later when nearly all of them had seen Jesus in that very room, they are still behind locked doors (John 20:19 & 26). But when this promise of Jesus is fulfilled at Pentecost in Acts 2, the disciples are transformed. When the Holy Spirit comes upon them, they really are given power from on high. Far from hiding behind locked doors, Peter stands up and bears witness about Jesus to a huge crowd who have gathered to see what is happening. Throughout Acts we find similar steps of bravery from the early Church. The power of the Spirit meant they weren't afraid to be witnesses of what they knew about Jesus even if it meant being thrown into prison or being killed.

One thing we see time and time again in the New Testament is that when the Holy Spirit fills people with power, they know about it. There's no one thing that shows someone has been filled with the Spirit; there's no one gift that stands as the litmus test, but when people are filled with the Holy Spirit they are changed. We all need to ask God to fill us with his Holy Spirit so that we too might know that power to be his witnesses.

To The End Of The Earth...

After Jesus has promised the disciples that he will give them power from on high by sending the Holy Spirit, he commissions them to be his witnesses 'in Jerusalem and in all Judea and Samaria, and to the end of the earth' (Acts 1:8). At this point the disciples were in Jerusalem. Judea was the wider area, mainly to the south of Jerusalem, and Samaria was another province just above Jerusalem. The phrase 'to the end of the earth' was probably simply meant to designate the rest of the world. Jesus commissions them to be his witnesses first where they are, then in the surrounding areas and then across the whole earth, much like circles getting bigger and bigger working out from a middle point.

The rest of Acts shows the disciples doing just this. They start in Jerusalem, move out into Judea and Samaria and then go off across the known world. As they do so, they plant churches. In each locality they bear witness to what they've seen and what they've come to understand, and when they have a core of believers in a certain place they establish a church. Not a special building or set of activities but a group of people who become a family and come together to worship Jesus and to help each other live as witnesses to what they have come to know is true. These churches were started by or with the help of apostles – leaders who work to see the truth about Jesus declared everywhere and churches firmly established there. In each church a team of elders was appointed to lead and care for the people. It's important to see that it was through the planting of local churches that the disciples sought to fulfil Jesus' commission to 'make disciples of all nations' (Matthew 28:19). Church and mission aren't separate; the Church is how God's kingdom will extend to the end of the earth.

The new churches we see established in Acts became involved in witnessing to their local areas, their friends, families and neighbours, but through prayer, finance and sometimes travelling long distances (a much harder task than it is today) they were also involved in witnessing to those in the surrounding regions and across the nations to the end of the earth.

Our call as Christians is still to be witnesses in our local areas, our countries and across the nations. All of us are called to be witnesses, but what that means will look different for each of us. Some of us will be called to be witnesses in our local areas; even the most normal day-to-day life can be used to be a witness for Jesus. Some of us will be called to be witnesses in different areas of our nations, to move to a different town or city to join an existing church or be involved in planting a new one. Again there, day-to-day life will be the way we can be witnesses for Jesus. Others of us will be called to be witnesses in other nations. It might be costly and mean leaving behind friends, family and job security; it might require hard work to learn new languages and cultures, but it's about being a witness for Jesus, being on the mission of God. As Christians our lives belong to God and his mission. We need to be listening to him, seeing where he wants us to be witnesses for him.

Wherever we are, we are all ultimately called to do the same thing. Witnessing doesn't have to be as hard as we make it. We've experienced something and come to recognise the truth; all we have to do is share that with others. We won't have all the right answers to people's questions but that's not a problem; we can still be Jesus' witnesses by sharing what we do know.

Identity Check-Up

Here are some questions and activities to help you perform an identity check-up.

Understanding Your Identity

Read Luke 24:44-49 and Acts 1:6-11 and think about these questions.
- What are the two meanings of being a 'witness'? (Luke 24:48; Acts 1:8)
- What had the disciples witnessed? (Luke 24:44-47)
- How does Jesus promise to help the disciples to be witnesses? (Acts 1:8)
- How did the disciples act on Jesus' commission to them to be witnesses? Where does the Church fit in?

Living Your Identity

Take some time to think about these questions or discuss them with others.

- What does the idea of 'witnessing' mean to you? Has this chapter challenged that?
- What are we witnesses to as Christians in the 21st century?
- Who can you be a witness to?
- What do we need to help us be witnesses? How should we pursue that?

Growing In Your Identity

Everyone loves a good story and all Christians have a good story. If you've become a Christian you have a fantastic story about what God has done for you. Even if you think your story is nothing special, it really is. It's a story of unstoppable love, outrageous forgiveness and eternal hope. Of finding what you were made for and being given everything, for doing nothing.

Think about your own story and jot down some ideas about what you would say if you had a few minutes to witness to a friend or family member. There might be lots of exciting things you could talk about, but remember that at the heart of it all is the fact that God has forgiven you and promised you an eternity with him in his perfect new creation. You can't guarantee your friend that if they become a Christian this life will be fantastic in every way (in fact, as we'll soon see, becoming a Christian guarantees you will experience suffering in this life), but you can guarantee that God wants to forgive them so they can enjoy eternity with him. That's why the place to focus is the core truth of the Gospel.

Spend some time praying that God would give you opportunities to witness about what God has done for you and ask him to give you his power from on high to help you.

Chapter 8

You Are... A Member Of The Body Of Christ

[12]For just as the body is one and has many members, and all the members of the body, though many, are one body, so it is with Christ. [13]For in one Spirit we were all baptized into one body—Jews or Greeks, slaves or free—and all were made to drink of one Spirit.

[14]For the body does not consist of one member but of many. [15]If the foot should say, "Because I am not a hand, I do not belong to the body," that would not make it any less a part of the body. [16]And if the ear should say, "Because I am not an eye, I do not belong to the body," that would not make it any less a part of the body. [17]If the whole body were an eye, where would be the sense of hearing? If the whole body were an ear, where would be the sense of smell? [18]But as it is, God arranged the members in the body, each one of them, as he chose. [19]If all were a single member, where would the body be? [20]As it is, there are many parts, yet one body.

> *²⁷Now you are the body of Christ and individually members of it. ²⁸And God has appointed in the church first apostles, second prophets, third teachers, then miracles, then gifts of healing, helping, administrating, and various kinds of tongues. ²⁹Are all apostles? Are all prophets? Are all teachers? Do all work miracles? ³⁰Do all possess gifts of healing? Do all speak with tongues? Do all interpret? ³¹But earnestly desire the higher gifts.*
>
> 1 Corinthians 12:12-20, 27-31

A Running Nose

Did you ever see the TV advert a few years ago which featured a family of characters who were all giant noses, with a couple of puny looking legs holding up their massive nose-bodies? Nothing else – just a giant nose and a couple of tiny legs. I think it was an advert for medication to relieve cold and flu symptoms. Anyway, I found it annoying. I'm not very good at the whole suspension of disbelief thing. All I could think every time I saw that advert were things like, 'How are those tiny legs holding up such a big body?', 'Why aren't they constantly bumping into things if they've got no eyes?' and 'How are these giant runny noses going to take this medicine when they've got no arms or hands to pick it up with?'. I don't think I'd get very far in the world of advertising.

The Apostle Paul was never subjected to that advert but I think he might have asked some similar questions. He had the idea of a nose-body, an eye-body or an ear-body thousands of years before that company did and he recognised that such a body would be useless. A body needs its many different parts to make up the whole. And so does the Church.

Now Concerning...

Do you ever worry that your church is a bit messy? Maybe sometimes you think that not everything's quite as it should be? Well don't worry – you're not the first. In 1 Corinthians Paul is writing to the church in Corinth addressing lots of worrying issues that he's heard about. The church is pretty messy, yet he still gives thanks to God for them (1 Corinthians 1:4). That should give us all some encouragement!

As well as addressing issues he's heard about, Paul responds to some questions the Corinthian Christians have sent him in a letter ('Now concerning the matters about which you wrote', 1 Corinthians 7:1). It seems some of these questions were about spiritual gifts, a topic Paul addresses in chapters 12-14 ('Now concerning', 1 Corinthians 12:1).

In chapter 12 he particularly focuses on the idea that though there are lots of different gifts and services and activities, they all come from the same God. They are all 'the work of one and the same Spirit, and he distributes them to each one, just as he determines' (1 Corinthians 12:11 NIV). It's at this point that he explains this further using the picture of a body.

One Body, Many Parts

Take a look at your body for a moment. How many parts does it have? How many bodies is it?

We all have one body but that one body is made up of many parts. We have a head and feet, arms and legs, a heart, lungs, arteries, toes and much more. In fact, according to the *Terminologia Anatomica* (which gives the official, internationally recognised terms for human anatomy) there are more than 7500 different parts of the human body.[a] Paul tells us that it's the same with Christ, whose body we are baptised into (1 Corinthians 12:12-13), but before explaining this he pauses to have some fun with the one body, many parts idea.

First he observes that each part of the body is truly a part of it (1 Corinthians 12:15-16). It would be absurd for one part of our bodies (such as a foot) to conclude that because it is not something else (such as a hand) it isn't really part of the body. Both are equally part of the body because both are necessary to make up the whole. This would be a bit like saying a yellow Skittle sweet isn't really a Skittle because you can't 'taste the rainbow' in it. But that would be misunderstanding how you 'taste the rainbow' in Skittles: you need the whole pack made up of many different individual Skittles to get the full effect. Second, Paul notes that it is important that there are lots of different parts making up the one body or else there would be all sorts of functions and abilities missing. So, for example, if we were just one giant eye, though we might have very good eyesight, we wouldn't be able to hear anything. Imagine you were just a giant nose or a hand or a lung. You wouldn't be able to do much or interact with other people. Life would be pretty boring and pretty lonely. On their own the parts of our body are limited; we need all of them to work together (1 Corinthians 12:17).

Instead of these absurd alternatives, God has created our bodies so that they are made up of all the different parts we need, each able to perform its own role. Many parts, but one body (1 Corinthians 12:18-20).

---

[a]Source: American Association of Anatomists (www.anatomy.org).

You Are The Body Of Christ

All this leads up to the statement that 'all of you are the body of Christ, each an individual part' (1 Corinthians 12:27).[b] Christians are each an individual part which go together to make a whole, the body of Christ.

The body of Christ is the Church. The Church is not a place or an official organisation; it's a group of people linked together by faith in Christ. The Greek word used for the Church in the New Testament means 'an assembly (of people) or a gathering'.[c] It's a word that denotes people, not place. No use of the word in the New Testament is for a building; it's always about a group of people. It can be unhelpful when the buildings we meet in are referred to as 'church' because it makes us think of the Church as a building, when in fact it's a body made up of those who believe in Christ. We don't go to church; we are the Church.[d]

---

[b] Author's translation. ESV: 'Now you (pl.) are the body of Christ and individually members of it.'

[c] The Greek is *ekklēsia*. It was used always for groups of people, never for a place. When the Old Testament was translated into Greek in the few centuries before Jesus (a translation called the Septuagint or LXX) the word *ekklēsia* was used more than a hundred times, usually to translate the Hebrew *qāhāl* ('congregation'), the word used for the congregation of the people of God. Therefore, when Jesus and the early Church used *ekklēsia* for the new group of believers they were also claiming to be the continuation of the Old Testament people of God.

[d] The word, in both the Greek of the New Testament and its English equivalent, does have two senses though. One is 'the Church' (usually spelt with a capital) which denotes what is sometimes called the universal Church, i.e. all believers, everywhere. The second, 'a church' or 'the church in...' (without a capital) is one local group of believers. So, for example, the church in Corinth were a group of believers who were a local church and together with lots of other similar local churches made up the universal Church.

The idea of the Church as a body is quite common in the New Testament. In another of his letters Paul says that Christ 'is the head of the body, the church' (Colossians 1:18). If we are the body, Christ is the head. He is the first part, the most important part and the one to whom we should submit (Ephesians 5:24) and this body is constantly growing and developing to become more like him (Ephesians 4:15-16).

Being A Body

If we are the body of Christ then everything Paul has just told us about bodies in 1 Corinthians 12 is also true of the Church. The Church is made up of lots of people. We are all different and all receive different gifts and abilities from God. Just as it would be absurd for a part of our human body to declare itself not to be a part of the body because it is different from other parts, so it is absurd to class ourselves or another Christian as not being a part of the body of Christ just because we have different giftings. Likewise, if we are a single body made of many parts, then just like our human bodies we need all the different parts in order to function properly as a whole. If we all just had gifts of healing, we would be very limited in what we could do. Likewise if we all had gifts of teaching we might have some great sermons but not much else. As a body we need the variety of parts to make up the one whole.

This means that churches should be communities where we embrace each other's differences, especially in terms of the gifting and roles God gives us; communities where individuals can be themselves and yet together be one body in Christ.

The Arrangement Of The Body

We know that a body needs all its different parts but there's something else that's important, and that's how those parts are put together. If I bought all the parts needed to make a car but then put them together in the wrong way, the car wouldn't be much use to me. Just having the parts isn't enough; they need to be put together correctly. Thankfully for the body of Christ, God gives out his gifts and puts them in the right places. He arranges the body.

Paul gives some examples of these different gifts and roles that God gives to Christians. This is one of several such lists in the New Testament.[e] There are two factors that show that something is a spiritual gift. First, as we mentioned at the beginning of this chapter, they are all empowered by the Holy Spirit: 'All these [gifts] are empowered by one and the same Spirit' (1 Corinthians 12:11). Even if the gift is something that might have some basis in natural ability, such as teaching, the Spirit helps, grows and empowers these abilities to fulfil God's purposes. The second factor is that they are all 'for the common good' (1 Corinthians 12:7); they are to build up the body of Christ to maturity (Ephesians 4:12-16). That means spiritual gifts are really important. For one thing, they're not just for fun but have an important role, and for another they are vital for the Church to reach the maturity God wants for her.

However, not everyone thinks we should expect spiritual gifts today. The gifts have been a big point of debate as some people claim that they were only ever meant for the short time period before the New Testament was written, to help people until they

---

[e] Similar lists are found in 1 Corinthians 12:7-10; Romans 12:6-8; Ephesians 4:7-13; 1 Peter 4:10-11.

had the last instalment of the Bible. When we take a careful look, though, we see that this goes completely against what the Bible tells us. Those who claim we shouldn't expect spiritual gifts today often argue from 1 Corinthians 13, which tells us that 'when the perfect comes' the gifts, such as prophecy, will cease. Some people believe 'when the perfect comes' (1 Corinthians 13:10) refers to the finishing of the New Testament. However, when we read on we see that that time will be like seeing God and the truth about him 'face to face' (1 Corinthians 13:12). Now, the New Testament is a fantastic gift from God which helps us to know him better and understand something of what he has done for us in Christ, but it can hardly be compared to seeing God 'face to face'. That moment will only come when Jesus returns. Clearly 'the perfect' has not yet come, so we should still expect to receive spiritual gifts from God.

Another important point is that spiritual gifts are given to build up the Church 'to mature manhood, to the measure of the stature of the fullness of Christ' (Ephesians 4:13). I don't know of any churches or Christians about whom we could say that yet. If the Church hasn't yet reached maturity, then we should surely expect the gifts given to help her reach that point to continue today.

After listing eight of the many gifts God shares among members of the body of Christ, Paul asks, 'Are all teachers? Do all work miracles? Do all possess gifts of healing?' (1 Corinthians 12:29-30). The obvious answer he's fishing for is a simple 'No'. Rather, some will be teachers, others will work miracles, others will have gifts of healing and still others will have different gifts. The body needs all the individual parts, whom God individually gifts and arranges.

Earnestly Desire

What's Paul's conclusion to this? 'Earnestly desire the higher gifts' (1 Corinthians 12:31). This might seem like a slightly weird conclusion given what he's already said. Why should we desire the gifts if it's God who chooses who to give them to and does the giving? And how can Paul talk about higher gifts, as if there's some sort of hierarchy, when he's just shown that each member and their individual gifts are vital for the whole body?

It seems the answer to these questions comes in chapter 14. There Paul says, 'Pursue love, and earnestly desire the spiritual gifts, especially that you may prophesy' (1 Corinthians 14:1). Prophecy, he says, is especially to be desired. The reason for this is given in the rest of the chapter. He explains that prophecy builds up the Church (1 Corinthians 14:4). The Church can understand the words of a prophecy and so be encouraged and helped by them. By contrast, a tongue only builds up the one who speaks it since it can't be understood by others (1 Corinthians 14:4). Indeed, it is for this reason that Paul insists if a tongue is brought in a public setting then an interpretation (a summary of what it means) must also be brought (1 Corinthians 14:13). When Paul encourages the Corinthians to desire the 'higher gifts' at the end of chapter 12 then, what he means is those that are best going to build up the Church. After all, that is the purpose of the gifts. It's also important to note that chapter 14 starts with the command, 'Pursue love'. Chapter 13 is inserted between the discussion about gifts in chapters 12 and 14 to remind the Corinthians that all of this needs to be built on a life of love. Without love, the spiritual gifts are pointless.

And what does he mean by 'earnestly desire'? What do you earnestly desire? Happiness? Safety and security for your family?

Money? Fun? How does earnestly desiring those things make you act? If we really want something, that normally motivates us to do something about it. It's the same with spiritual gifts.

It's true that God is the one who gives the gifts and that he will choose what he gives to whom, but that doesn't mean we're not involved at all. God loves to hear and respond to our requests. He loves to see us eagerly desiring to use spiritual gifts to build up his Church. We need to show God that we are willing and wanting to receive and use his gifts. If I had a brand new piece of technology which could do amazing things to help people, I wouldn't just give it to the first person I saw; I would wait to see who genuinely wanted to use it to help others. In the same way God will respond as a father who loves to give good gifts to his children when we seek spiritual gifts, asking him to grow them in us.

The other part of this is that none of the gifts are things that take us over as if we have no say and no control. Don't expect just because it is God who gives the gifts that one day you will wake up and like some remote control robot speak a prophecy to someone or explain a tricky piece of the Bible. To use the gifts, we have to do stuff. We have to deliberately listen and speak and pray and study and serve. We express our earnest desire for the gifts by using them. Try things out. It doesn't matter if sometimes we get things wrong or if people aren't healed when we pray for them. God will love seeing that we want to use his gifts, and then he'll give us more.

So the key to earnestly desiring the gifts of the Spirit, to play our part as members of the body of Christ, is to pray and do. So go on, what are you waiting for?

Identity Check-Up

Here are some questions and activities to help you perform an identity check-up.

Understanding Your Identity

Read 1 Corinthians 12:12-31 and think about these questions.
- In what way is the Church like a human body?
- How have we become part of this body? (v.13)
- What is God's role in the body of the Church? (v.18)
- What does it mean to 'earnestly desire the higher gifts'? (v.31)

Living Your Identity

Take some time to think about these questions or discuss them with others.
- Do you think of yourself as a vital part of the body of Christ? If not, why not?
- What impact should the truths in this chapter have on our churches and on our relationships with others within our churches?
- What gifts do you feel God has given you, or do others recognise in you? Are you using them to play your part in the body?
- Do you earnestly desire the higher gifts? How can we grow in our use of the gifts?

Growing In Your Identity

A healthy body has two eyes. However, for those eyes to be of benefit to the whole body, they need to be open, ready to see and report information to the brain. In the same way, God gives us all gifts to use for the benefit of the body, but we still have to take steps to use them. Sometimes we can get into thinking that because these gifts are from God and are called 'spiritual', we're not very involved and we have to wait for God to take us over so we become like a puppet in his hand and use his gifts. The reality, however, is that God gives us the gifts and wants to partner with us in their use. Using the gifts doesn't just happen. We don't need to wait for God to take us over. He's waiting for us to take up the gifts he has given us and to use them.

Take some time to think about what spiritual gifts you think God has already given you (you might find it helpful to look at the lists of gifts in 1 Corinthians 12:7-10, 28, Romans 12:6-8, Ephesians 4:7-13 and 1 Peter 4:10-11).

What gifts would you like to have and use to benefit the body that you don't already have? Take some time to ask God for them. It's good to be regularly praying for certain gifts God puts on our heart.

Start a spiritual gifts diary. Make a record each time you use a spiritual gift. Do this for a few weeks and look back on it, thinking about the questions above.

CHAPTER 9

You Are... A Temple Of The Holy Spirit

^{12}"All things are lawful for me," but not all things are helpful. "All things are lawful for me," but I will not be dominated by anything. ^{13}"Food is meant for the stomach and the stomach for food"—and God will destroy both one and the other. The body is not meant for sexual immorality, but for the Lord, and the Lord for the body. ^{14}And God raised the Lord and will also raise us up by his power. ^{15}Do you not know that your bodies are members of Christ? Shall I then take the members of Christ and make them members of a prostitute? Never! ^{16}Or do you not know that he who is joined to a prostitute becomes one body with her? For, as it is written, "The two will become one flesh." ^{17}But he who is joined to the Lord becomes one spirit with him. ^{18}Flee from sexual immorality. Every other sin a person commits is outside the body, but the sexually immoral person sins against his own body. ^{19}Or do you not know that your body is a temple of the Holy Spirit within you, whom you have from God? You are not your *own, [20] for you were bought with a price. So glorify God in your body.*

1 Corinthians 6:12-20

Knowing Where You Are

We've all got that friend or relative who has the most perfect, pristinely kept house. Each time you walk through that door you feel your blood pressure rise a few notches. The shoes come straight off, messy foods are to be avoided and red wine is out of the question! It's always a slightly nerve-wracking experience, even if you know the friend or family member really does love you. The fact that you know it's their house and it's important to them matters; it affects how you behave when you're there.

If that's how we act around relatives and friends, imagine how we should act around a holy God. That's the idea Paul expresses when he tells the Corinthians to remember what they are.

More Mess At Corinth

We live in a sex-saturated world. Everywhere we go we are surrounded by sex. For many people sex is a god. Just think about advertising: whether it be on TV, on billboards or in shop windows, sex is used to sell just about anything. Perfume, cars, clothes, jewellery, even yoghurt is advertised with some reference or allusion to sexual pleasure. Nearly every TV show or film includes a storyline which is ultimately about the quest for sex. In our modern Western society sex is something people aspire to; TV, films and music are just a window into this larger quest.

A lot of us tend to think that this sex obsession is a modern thing. True, the so-called 'Sexual Revolution' of the 1960s was a major part of our journey to the current climate, but it's far from being a modern problem. All throughout history sex has been a god for many people. This was no less true in the ancient world in which Jesus and the New Testament authors lived. One of the most sex-saturated places in the ancient world was Corinth, where there was a church to whom Paul wrote several letters.

Corinth was an important city in Greece, a centre for trade through which many people travelled. It was also one of the worst cities in the world. The city had such a bad reputation because of the immorality which characterised it that the word *Korinthiazein* (i.e. to live like a Corinthian) became a term for living a life of immorality. Towering over the city was the huge Temple of Aphrodite, Greek goddess of love. In that temple were more than a thousand sacred prostitutes, with whom men would have sex to connect with Aphrodite. Also in Corinth was the Temple of Apollo, another of the Greek gods, seen as the perfection of male beauty. At the Temple of Apollo male worshippers showed their devotion through sexual acts with young males. Corinth was a sex-obsessed city. Sex was idolised as a god, just as it is in our modern culture.

So it should be no surprise to us when we find that some of the mess Paul has heard about in Corinth involves sexual immorality. At the end of chapter 6 Paul gives a whole host of reasons why and how as Christians we should flee from sexual immorality.[a]

---

[a] What do we mean by sexual immorality? Sexual immorality, as the Bible talks about it, is any sexual act which takes place outside of a marriage relationship between a man and a woman. It covers sex before marriage, adultery, homosexual acts, incest and lust (Matthew 5:27-28). The word Paul uses for sexual immorality is *porneia*, from which we get the word 'pornography'.

Lawful But Not Good

What's your favourite slogan? 'Every little helps'? 'You can lead a horse to water, but you can't make it drink'? 'Don't throw the baby out with the bathwater'?

It seems some of the Corinthians had their own favourite slogan: 'All things are lawful for me' (1 Corinthians 6:12). It might even have been something Paul had said to them: we've already seen that as Christians we are free from condemnation and from the law, no longer under its judgements. This was a slogan that some of the Corinthians had been using to justify sexual immorality. Perhaps it had reached Paul's ears through those who had told him about what was occurring in Corinth.

Sexual immorality was a big problem in the church in Corinth. Paul has already addressed reports of incest in the church (1 Corinthians 5:1-2) and mentioned those who are sexually immoral or practice homosexual acts as examples of people who will not inherit the kingdom of God (1 Corinthians 6:9).

Though the slogan might fit with some of Paul's other teaching, he carefully adds two qualifications which help us begin to understand what Christian freedom really is. First he says that though all things may be lawful for a Christian, 'not all things are helpful' (1 Corinthians 6:12). Just because we can do something, it doesn't always mean it's a good idea. True freedom is the freedom to do what is truly best for us and for others. So when we're thinking about whether we should do something or not, one thing to ask is, 'Is that actually going to be good and helpful for me and for others?'

Paul's second qualification is that he 'will not be enslaved by anything' (1 Corinthians 6:12). In *You Are... Dead to Sin* we saw that we were once enslaved to sin; it had a power over us we couldn't get away from. But by dying and rising with Christ we are freed from that slavery and instead become slaves of God. It would be crazy for us now to allow something else to have power and control over us. That would be going from freedom back to oppressive slavery. So the second thing we should ask ourselves when considering what to do is, 'Will that take hold of me and reduce my freedom?'

True freedom isn't about being able to do absolutely anything. True freedom is the ability to be who we were created to be. That means that true freedom comes when we live as God wants us to, doing what he designed us for and fleeing those things which go against that design.

Paul introduces another slogan from the Corinthian Christians: 'Food is meant for the stomach and the stomach for food' (1 Corinthians 6:13). This idea was probably taken from the Greek thought which would have surrounded these early Christians. Some Greek thinkers believed that the body was like a prison in which the soul – the important bit – was trapped while on earth. If this is the case, what you do with your body is of little importance. So, they argued, it doesn't matter what you eat – just enjoy it, go wild. If this was true, they could then argue the same for sex. Just as many people today say that sex is just biology – just enjoy it, go wild. But Paul doesn't share this view. Food and the stomach will both be destroyed by God. They aren't important. But the body as a whole, that's a different matter. 'The body is not meant for sexual immorality, but for the Lord, and the Lord for the body' (1 Corinthians 6:13). God made our bodies to be for him, devoted to him. True freedom is about living in the way we were created to be. So true freedom is living not in sexual immorality but in utter devotion to God.

5 Reasons To Flee From Sexual Immorality

The internet is full of 'Top 5...' lists. You can find the 'Top 5 Most Beautiful Landscapes', the 'Top 5 Best Cat Beards', even the 'Top 5 Classic Song Lyrics Significantly Improved By Cats'! In 1 Corinthians 6 Paul gives us his own 'Top 5' list: the 'Top 5 Reasons Why Christians Should Flee From Sexual Immorality'.

In at number 5 comes *our future resurrection*: 'God raised the Lord and will also raise us up by his power' (1 Corinthians 6:14). Jesus was killed on a cross and laid in a tomb, but God raised him up from the dead to a new resurrection life. The promise of the Gospel is that God will one day do the same for all Christians. God is in the business of renewing all things, undoing all the mess that has entered the world through human sin. Part of that mess is death, and God will one day destroy death and raise us up to eternal life in a perfect new creation (take a look at 1 Corinthians 15). If this is so, then the Greek thinkers who claimed the body is just a prison trapping the soul were clearly wrong. Your body is important because God will one day renew it so it's perfect. We need to value our bodies as much as God does.

Number 4 is *our place as a member of the body of Christ* (1 Corinthians 6:15-17). We've already seen (in *You Are... A Member of the Body of Christ*) that as Christians we are each an important part of a wider whole, the body of Christ. Paul reminds the Corinthians that to have sex with someone is to become one flesh with them, just as God declared in Genesis 2. But it is completely inappropriate for a part of the body of Christ to become one flesh with a prostitute. The example of a prostitute is chosen here because of the many temple prostitutes in Corinth. Perhaps some of the Christians there had still been visiting these prostitutes even after turning to Christ. 'Prostitute' could be replaced by any individual who is not the other's spouse. Far from becoming 'one flesh' with a prostitute, believers should be 'joined to the Lord' and be 'one spirit with him' (1 Corinthians 6:17).

Coming in at number 3 in Paul's 'Top 5 Reasons to Flee Sexual Immorality' is *the self-abuse of sexual immorality*. 'Every other sin a person commits is outside the body, but the sexually immoral person sins against his own body' (1 Corinthians 6:18). When we get involved in sexual immorality we are putting our bodies to a use they're not designed for. It's like throwing a fish into a field rather than a lake; it will ultimately be uncomfortable and damaging. When we realise that sexual immorality is actually a form of self-abuse, we are able to see how absurd it is.

Number 2 is that fact that *we are all temples of the Holy Spirit* (1 Corinthians 6:19). What does that mean? A temple is a place where a god lives. As we mentioned earlier, there were two big temples in Corinth – one to Aphrodite and one to Apollos. They were places where people believed the gods dwelt and where they would go to worship them.

The Jews, the people of God in the Old Testament, were unique in that they always had only one temple at a time, where the living God would dwell among them. First this was the tabernacle – a sort of tent – while they lived in the wilderness (Exodus 40:34-38), and later it was the temple in Jerusalem (1 Kings 8:10-11; 2 Chronicles 7:1-3). These temples were the place where the real God actually chose to live on earth and where his people could meet with him and worship him. Because God was there, they were places of great holiness. To be holy is to be separate or other and completely incompatible with sin. The temple was the place where the holy God lived on earth.

When Jesus died on the cross the curtain in the temple which separated the most holy part where God dwelt and the rest of the building was torn from top to bottom (Mark 15:38). God would no longer live in that man-made temple. He now lives in each and every Christian believer. We are now the place where God chooses to dwell on earth. The holy God, the one who is completely incompatible with sin, lives in us. If that's the case, how can we let our bodies be involved in any form of sexual immorality?

Finally, at number 1, *we don't own our bodies*. Modern culture tells us that our bodies are our own and so we can do what we like with them. We can have sex with whomever we want, whenever we want, because it's 'my body and my choice'. But for the Christian that is completely wrong. Paul cuts right through that sort of thinking, telling us, 'You are not your own.' How come? 'For you were bought with a price' (1 Corinthians 6:19-20). God has purchased you for himself at the cost of his son. We were once slaves to sin but through the death and resurrection of Jesus we are bought out of that slavery. As we saw in *You Are... Dead to Sin*, that doesn't leave us aimlessly walking around on our own. Rather we are taken out of slavery to sin to become slaves of God (Romans 6:16-22). We don't own our bodies. It is not our right to decide what to do with them. Just as the slaves who were bought at a price in the ancient world then belonged to their new masters, we now belong to a new master, God. But God is a good master and this slavery is actually true freedom. By obeying our new master in how we use our bodies, we will enter that freedom.

Glorify God In Your Body

All this leads Paul to the conclusion: 'So glorify God in your body' (1 Corinthians 6:20). As Christians we are to worship God even in the way we use the bodies he has given us. What we do with them matters, big time.

The couple of verses before this passage are really important too. If I went to the ultra-clean and tidy house of my relative and amidst the joy of a family gathering I knocked over a glass of red wine, I would have good reason to be scared. But when we slip up as Christians, we don't need to be scared. Before Paul gives us his Top 5 list, he reminds us of the glorious truth of the Gospel. Having given a list of sinful actions, headlined by sexual immorality, he tells us, 'Some of you were once like that. But you were cleansed; you were made holy; you were made right with God by calling on the name of the Lord Jesus Christ and by the Spirit of our God' (1 Corinthians 6:11 NLT).

If we make a mess in God's house, we don't have to be scared because he's got the best cleaner in the universe. But he wants his house to be pristine so we can enjoy it in all its beauty. So let's glorify God in our bodies, remembering that we are each a temple of the Holy Spirit.

Identity Check-Up

Here are some questions and activities to help you perform an identity check-up.

Understanding Your Identity

Read 1 Corinthians 6:12-20 and think about these questions.
- How should we respond to the claim that 'all things are lawful for us'? (v.12)
- What are Paul's top 5 reasons to flee sexual immorality?
- What is a temple?
- Why is it significant that we are temples of the Holy Spirit?

Living Your Identity

Take some time to think about these questions or discuss them with others.
- Do you ever say or think something similar to 'But all things are lawful for me'? What should we remind ourselves when we have these thoughts?
- How can we apply Paul's 'Top 5 Reasons Why Christians Should Flee Sexual Immorality' to our lives in practical ways? What sort of things do we need to do and constantly remind ourselves?
- What are the real danger areas in your life where you need to be on your guard and ready to flee sexual immorality?
- How does the truth of 1 Corinthians 6:11 encourage us in our battle against sexual immorality?

Growing In Your Identity

Regardless of who we are and what our lives are currently like, we all need to be on guard against sexual immorality. Some stuff Jesus said can help us here.

> And lead us not into temptation,
> but deliver us from evil.
>
> Matthew 6:13

> And if your hand or your foot causes you to sin, cut it off and throw it away. It is better for you to enter life crippled or lame than with two hands or two feet to be thrown into the eternal fire. And if your eye causes you to sin, tear it out and throw it away. It is better for you to enter life with one eye than with two eyes to be thrown into the hell of fire.
>
> Matthew 18:8-9

Pre-empt The Problem

Jesus was serious about sin. He told us to be constantly praying that God would protect us from temptation and to be proactive about dealing with sin.

We all need to be constantly aware of this battle. Even if you don't think this is something you're struggling with right now, you need to be fighting the battle. The point at which you think you're safe is the point at which you are actually most vulnerable to the enemy's attacks.

Preparing In Prayer

How often do you pray that God would protect you from temptation? Don't wait till it happens; pray regularly for God's help in this area. You can start that now.

Preparing In Action

Take some time to think about your life. Where are the danger points? Where do you end up looking at things you shouldn't or having thoughts you shouldn't? If the devil was going to catch you out in this area, where would it be?

Sex is everywhere and you don't have to seek out certain places or media to be presented with it. Count how many times a day you are presented with sexually provocative images or speech and you will be amazed.

Isolate your danger points and take some action. If it's TV adverts, learn to look away or go and get a drink while they're on. If it's catalogues, tear out and throw away the problem pages as soon as it arrives so they can't pose a threat to you. If the internet, get a filter or start being accountable with a friend. If loneliness or emotional pain, run to God for his healing and share with Christian friends who can support you. Know when you're vulnerable and how you'll fight in those times.

If you knew you were going to be in a battle, you wouldn't wait until the enemy started attacking before you thought about your battle strategies or began to gather your equipment. It should be no different with our battle against sin. Make sure you're prepared.

Get Serious About Sin

If you're struggling with sexual immorality now, get serious with it. Choose to do something about it. Attack the problem at its source. Bring it to God and ask him to help you to change your behaviour and share with a church leader or a trusted Christian friend who can walk through the battle with you.

CHAPTER 10

You Are... Part Of A Holy Priesthood

⁴As you come to him, a living stone rejected by men but in the sight of God chosen and precious, ⁵you yourselves like living stones are being built up as a spiritual house, to be a holy priesthood, to offer spiritual sacrifices acceptable to God through Jesus Christ ... ⁹But you are a chosen race, a royal priesthood, a holy nation, a people for his own possession, that you may proclaim the excellencies of him who called you out of darkness into his marvelous light. ¹⁰Once you were not a people, but now you are God's people; once you had not received mercy, but now you have received mercy.
1 Peter 2:4-5, 9-10

Direct Access

Access All Areas. Three little words with a lot of power. A few years back I was serving at a Christian festival and because of my role I had an 'Access All Areas' pass. I could go anywhere I wanted on site. That little pass meant I could get into any venue, get past any steward and skip any queue. But it also came with some responsibility. I hadn't been given that pass so I could sit around looking at it all day, thinking how nice it is to have 'Access All Areas'. I had been given it because I was there to perform a role. I had to use it to do the job I was there to do.

As Christians we've also been given an 'Access All Areas' pass, and with that pass we receive a role to perform.

Living In Tension

How do you live in a world where the majority of people think differently to you, where you're being attacked because you're different and life is just really tough? Well that's the sort of question Peter was seeking to answer when he wrote to the Christians in five regions of the Roman Empire about 30 years after Jesus had returned to be with his father.

When Peter wrote to these Christians who were being persecuted because of their faith, he kept pointing them to who they were and where they were headed. When they faced difficult times in the present, they needed to know why they were able to endure it and the better hope the future held for them.

A Spiritual House

One of my favourite games is Jenga. In Jenga you build a tower of little wooden blocks and then one by one each player has to carefully remove one of the blocks without making the tower fall down. Some pieces come out easily; others turn out to be vital to the tower's stability and the whole thing comes crashing down when someone tries to remove them.

In his letter Peter uses the image of a building made of lots of stones. He says that both Jesus and Christians are like 'living stones'. Jesus is a living stone 'rejected by men but in the sight of God chosen and precious' (1 Peter 2:4). While he was on earth Jesus was rejected by humanity and executed on a Roman cross. But God raised him from the dead – that's why he's a *living* stone. Now that he has ascended to be with his father, many people still reject him, but to God he is still chosen and precious.

Peter tells us that when we come to Jesus we are also like living stones and 'are being built up as a spiritual house' (1 Peter 2:5). Just like those vital pieces in the Jenga tower, Jesus is the vital part of God's new house and builds the rest of us together to complete the house. In the ancient world the word 'house' could be used for a temple which, as we saw in the last chapter, was the dwelling place (or house) of a god (e.g. 1 Kings 5:1-6; Luke 6:4). The fact that Peter calls this house 'spiritual' probably means he sees it as a temple for God, where he can dwell on earth, just as Paul says in 1 Corinthians 6. No longer does God live in a temple in Jerusalem, but in each individual believer.

Temples And Priests

But unlike Paul in 1 Corinthians, Peter doesn't stop there. He's got something else to tell us. Why are we being built into a spiritual house? 'To be a holy priesthood' (1 Peter 2:5). In the Old Testament the priests were men who were appointed to represent the people of Israel before God in the temple. They performed sacrifices on behalf of the people and were kind of the middle men between God and Israel. Israelites couldn't go directly to God; they needed a priest to mediate between them.

Now, though, all believers are members of this priesthood. That means we all have direct access to God. We no longer need priests to stand before God for us. Jesus has become our great high priest who has made open the way for us to come before God forever. 'Since we have a great high priest who has ascended into heaven, Jesus the Son of God, let us hold firmly to the faith we profess ... Let us then approach God's throne of grace with confidence, so that we may receive mercy and find grace to help us in our time of need' (Hebrews 4:14, 16 NIV).

Some Christian traditions still expect people to go to God through someone else, as if Christian leaders have replaced the Old Testament priests. But here Peter tells us that we are now all priests; we all have that right of access. Sometimes we don't feel like we do and we shy away from going to God, thinking that what we've done is too bad or that God doesn't really want to be in relationship with us, but that's when we need to remind ourselves that Jesus is our great high priest who has dealt with our sin once and for all, leaving us free from condemnation. Jesus has given us an 'Access All Areas' pass.

Playing A Role

Being a priest isn't just about having access; it's also about having a role. As we've mentioned, the priests in the Old Testament were responsible for carrying out the sacrifices and offerings necessary to provide cleansing for the people and to maintain their relationship with God and their purity as his holy people. As Christians living after Jesus, the sacrifice necessary to make up for our sins and make us pure has already been made, once and for all in Jesus (Hebrews 10:12-14). But we still have a role as priests – 'to offer spiritual sacrifices acceptable to God through Jesus Christ' (1 Peter 2:5).

But what are spiritual sacrifices? Even in the Old Testament sacrifice was sometimes used metaphorically to denote things like thanksgiving (Psalm 50:14), repentance (Psalm 51:17) and prayer (Psalm 141:2). This continued after the period of the Old Testament, especially when Jews didn't have access to the Temple. One group who removed themselves from wider Jewish society a little bit before the time of Jesus saw themselves as a human temple and talked about prayer as an acceptable sacrifice to God: 'And prayer rightly offered shall be as an acceptable fragrance of righteousness, and perfection of way as a delectable free-will offering'.[a]

To offer spiritual sacrifices, then, is to worship God. This doesn't just mean singing a few songs to him once a week; it means living a life devoted to him. Paul tells the Romans, 'offer your bodies as a living sacrifice, holy and pleasing to God—this is your true and proper worship' (Romans 12:1 NIV). Worship is a way of life. In everything we do we have a choice to do it in a way which honours and worships God or in a way which doesn't. As holy priests we are called to do all things as worship to God. The author of Hebrews writes, 'Let us offer through Jesus a continual sacrifice of praise to God, proclaiming our allegiance to his name. And don't forget to do good and to share with those in need. These are the sacrifices that please God' (Hebrews 13:15-16 NLT). He sees the spiritual sacrifices of God's new priesthood as both

---

[a] 1QS 10.5. 1QS, or *The Community Rule*, is a text from the library of the Qumran community, one of the Dead Sea Scrolls. Quote taken from Vermes, *The Complete Dead Sea Scrolls* (Penguin, 2004).

praise from our mouths and the act of doing good to others. Both are sacrifices which are pleasing to God.

Living As God's People

In verses 6-8 Peter goes on to contrast our position as living stones who have believed in the cornerstone, Jesus, with those who have rejected him and who 'stumble because they disobey the word' (1 Peter 2:8).

He then comes back to talking about us as a conclusion to this section. Verse 9 applies a list of descriptions originally applied to Israel in the Old Testament (Exodus 19:5-6; Deuteronomy 7:6; Isaiah 43:20-21) to Christians. Peter is not only telling his readers more about who they are as Christians but is also trying to show them that they stand in continuity with God's Old Testament people, even if they aren't Jews by birth.

Christians are 'a chosen race'. Just as Jesus was the 'chosen and precious' living stone (1 Peter 2:4), so Christians are a group who have been chosen by God (see *You Are... Chosen*). We are a 'royal priesthood'. Here Peter repeats the idea found in verse 5 but this time adds that this priesthood is royal. As priests we come to God, and God is king, so this makes us royal priests. Christians are 'a holy nation'. This is true in two senses. First we have each been made holy through the sacrifice of Jesus, and second we are all being made more and more holy in how we act through the work of the Holy Spirit within us. 'A people for his own possession'; as we've seen several times already, we have been taken out of slavery to sin and have become slaves to God. We are now subjects of the king, but subjects with an 'Access All Areas' pass.

All of these things are so that 'you may proclaim the excellencies of him who called you out of darkness into his marvelous light' (1 Peter 2:9). To proclaim God's excellencies could be an act of worship or an act of witnessing. When the word Peter has used here for 'proclaim' is used by the Greek translators of the Old Testament it is always about worship, not witnessing, so that is probably the focus here.[b] To proclaim God's excellencies is just another way of talking about the 'spiritual sacrifices' (1 Peter 2:5) we are to bring to God as his priests. The 'excellencies' are the amazing things God has done for us as Christians. He called us out of darkness – spiritual death, condemnation, slavery to sin and the law – and into his marvellous light – new life, forgiveness, adoption and freedom.

So to be part of the holy and royal priesthood of God is to have direct access to him and to use that access to worship him, giving him all the praise, glory and honour he deserves.

Identity Check-Up

Here are some questions and activities to help you perform an identity check-up.

Understanding Your Identity

Read 1 Peter 2:4-10 and think about these questions.
- What was the role of the Old Testament priests?
- What does it mean for us to be priests?
- What are 'spiritual sacrifices'? (v.5)

---

b The Greek word is *exangellō*. E.g. Psalm 79:13 '[We] will give thanks to you forever; from generation to generation we will recount [*exangellō*] your praise'; Psalm 107:22 'And let them offer sacrifices of thanksgiving, and tell [*exangellō*] of his deeds in songs of joy!'

- What does it mean to 'proclaim the excellencies of him who called you out of darkness into his marvelous light'? (v.9)

Living Your Identity

Take some time to think about these questions or discuss them with others.
- Do you live as if you really have constant, direct access to God? How can we help ourselves live out this truth?
- Do you think of yourself as offering spiritual sacrifices to God and proclaiming his excellencies?
- How should our role as a holy priesthood affect our daily lives?

Growing In Your Identity

Our role as priests is to offer spiritual sacrifices to God. The New Testament talks about spiritual sacrifices in several places. Look up these passages and see what they say about these sacrifices. Take some time to think about how much they feature in your life now and how you can perform them more as you live out your role as a member of God's holy priesthood.
- Romans 12:1-3
- Philippians 4:18
- Hebrews 13:15-16
- Revelation 8:1-5

Chapter 11

You Are... Salt And Light

^{13}"You are the salt of the earth, but if salt has lost its taste, how shall its saltiness be restored? It is no longer good for anything except to be thrown out and trampled under people's feet.

^{14}"You are the light of the world. A city set on a hill cannot be hidden. ^{15}Nor do people light a lamp and put it under a basket, but on a stand, and it gives light to all in the house. ^{16}In the same way, let your light shine before others, so that they may see your good works and give glory to your Father who is in heaven."

Matthew 5:13-16

Bring Back The Salt!

I know about salt losing its saltiness! When I was younger my family and I would often go swimming at the weekend. The highlight of these days (since I never really liked water all that much) was the trip over the road to McDonald's after we'd finished at the pool. And the highlight of being at McDonald's was the French fries (or more precisely, mixing the French fries and the strawberry milkshake!). However, when I went back to McDonald's recently, I was horrified to find my beloved French fries tasted nothing like I remembered. I thought maybe I had exaggerated how good they were in my memory. But then I discovered that due to today's healthy eating drive most of the salt which had made the fries I remember so tasty had been taken out. The fries had lost their saltiness, and with it, for me, a lot of their tastiness.

Keep It Salty

Salt has always been an important ingredient and it plays an important part in some of Jesus' teaching. Here we have Matthew's account of Jesus teaching his followers on the side of a mountain (often called the Sermon on the Mount). His teaching in Matthew 5-7 is all about how his followers should live in God's kingdom on earth. Within this teaching Jesus tells us two important things about who we are as Christians.

We mainly use salt to flavour our food. It's a powerful thing. Just a little salt can make a big difference. It's the sort of ingredient you often won't notice when it's there, but take it out and you'll soon realise something's missing. The same was true in the ancient world, but much more important was its use as a preservative. In a world where there were no fridges or freezers, rubbing a little salt into meat would slow down the process of decay. I might miss the salt on my French fries because I loved the taste, but if there had been a similar clampdown on salt usage in the ancient world, things would have been much more serious. Salt was important for preserving food and protecting people from getting ill by eating food that had gone off.

So when Jesus told his followers, 'You are the salt of the earth' (Matthew 5:13), they knew its significance. He meant that Christians are to have a preserving effect on society. In a world that is raging against God and his kingdom, we are called to be different, to have a positive influence, to bring his kingdom on earth as it is in heaven.

If salt loses its saltiness it's no good for anything.[a] All you can do with it is throw it away (Matthew 5:13). To be useful and play its role it has to retain its key qualities. Jesus tells us that the same is true of us as Christians. We are designed to have a positive effect in the world around us. But if we don't live as God wants us to, being examples of his kingdom on earth in what we say and what we do, we won't have that effect. In fact, to lose our saltiness is to make ourselves fools. The word Jesus uses for the salt losing its taste more commonly means 'to make foolish' (e.g. in Romans 1:22 and 1 Corinthians 1:20). If we let ourselves lose our saltiness, we are making ourselves fools. Society needs us to stand firm and retain our key qualities as subjects of God in order to preserve it and help it become better. God needs us to do this too. He gives us the privilege of being his representatives and ambassadors of his kingdom on earth (2 Corinthians 5:20).

One of the clearest examples of this is where the morality God wants is different from that which most people in the world follow. Some people think that the Church needs to change and

---

[a] Technically speaking salt can't lose its saltiness, but 'most salt in the ancient world derived from salt marshes or the like, rather than by evaporation of salt water, and therefore contained many impurities. The actual salt, being more soluble than the impurities, could be leached out, leaving a residue so dilute it was of little worth' (D.A. Carson, 'Matthew' in *The Expositor's Bible Commentary: Volume 8: Matthew, Mark, Luke* [Zondervan: 1984] p.138).

'get with the times' in cases like this. They argue that we need to keep up with the way society's opinions change or people will never respond to the Gospel. But Jesus would tell us exactly the opposite. As Christians we're meant to be different. And in our difference we will have a good effect upon those around us. When we hold to God's morality, not the world's, we are demonstrating and offering the way of life all people were made for. We stand as examples of true freedom, the freedom to be who we were designed to be. In this way we will be the salt of the earth, preserving it from destroying itself even more and presenting it with a better way of living – the way of living we were designed for.

Let Your Light Shine

Jesus then switches metaphors to continue his point. 'You are the light of the world' (Matthew 5:14). In the Old Testament God tells his chosen servant, 'I will make you as a light for the nations, that my salvation may reach to the end of the earth' (Isaiah 49:6). This was fulfilled in Jesus, who came to earth as God's chosen servant and declared, 'I am the light of the world' (John 8:12; also Matthew 4:16). As those 'in Christ' we also take on this role: we are to be God's lights going out into the world: 'Do all things without grumbling or questioning, that you may be blameless and innocent, children of God without blemish in the midst of a crooked and twisted generation, among whom you shine as lights in the world' (Philippians 2:14-15).

Lights are meant to shine. 'A city set on a hill cannot be hidden' (Matthew 5:14). In the ancient world urban buildings were often made of white limestone which would reflect the sun during the day and so shine brightly. At night the use of lamps all across the city would cast a glow visible even to those quite a way away; just as if you go out into the countryside at night today and look towards a town or city you'll see the glow of the street lamps. So an ancient city was very hard to miss and almost impossible to hide. 'Nor do people light a lamp and put it under a basket, but on a stand, and it gives light to all in the house' (Matthew 5:15). Since there were no electric lights in Jesus' day, people had to use lamps. When lamps were lit they were placed on a stand to raise them up and maximise the spread of their light across the room. To put a basket over such a lamp would be absurd; it would completely defeat the point of lighting it in the first place.

The same is true, Jesus says, of us. If we are the light of the world, why would we stop people from seeing that light? 'In the same way, let your light shine before others, so that they may see your good works and give glory to your Father who is in heaven' (Matthew 5:16). Just as a city is always visible and a lamp is lit to let it shine brightly, so we are to let our light shine brightly so that all people can see it.

As Christians we are meant to be visible. We're not meant to withdraw from the world into some secret, protected bubble; we're meant to go out into the world and show others what God is like. Our light is our good conduct which God wants people to see so they will worship him.

If you go for a walk at night and you see a light in the distance you know there is something there. Light doesn't just appear; it always has a source. In the same way, when people see that Christians are different, they'll know that there must be something different about the source. Our good deeds are a way of showing people what God is really like and what he does for people.

Being Salt and Light

There are lots of practical things which come out of this truth. First, as we've already said, Christians need to be out in the world, not hiding from it. Don't cover up your light; shine it in people's eyes!

Second, we need to make sure that we keep our light shining and don't let it become extinguished or weakened. We are God's representatives and so we need to flee from everything that would give him a bad name. We are his representatives on earth and we need to take that seriously. If people know you are a Christian but all they see coming from you is darkness, you are hindering God's mission. Make sure you are displaying a pure light.

Third, we need to be clear about the source of our light. We aren't different because we're trying to be good people – that's not the Gospel, even if it's from the right heart of wanting to love God. We are different because God has made us different. We were once in darkness but the great light of the world has now made us lights too. If people ask us about the source of our light we need to make sure that all the focus is put on God. All light has a source; we can't make it by our own power. Likewise no one can change by themselves; we all need God to change us. So let your light shine, that people might see and come to worship the source of that light.

Identity Check-Up

Here are some questions and activities to help you perform an identity check-up.

Understanding Your Identity

Read Matthew 5:13-16 and think about these questions.
- What was the main use of salt in Jesus' day?
- How should we be like salt?
- What does the imagery of light suggest about our role in the world?
- How should we use our light? (v.16)

Living Your Identity

Take some time to think about these questions or discuss them with others.
- In what ways can you be salt in your day-to-day life?
- What might stop you from fulfilling your role as 'the salt of the earth'?
- In what ways should we be like lights in the world?
- What do we need to do to make sure our light isn't hidden?

Growing In Your Identity

Jesus says that we should let our light shine so that others might see our good works and give glory to God. Sometimes, if people notice there is something different about us, it's easy to either chicken out of telling them that our good works are the fruit of God's work in us or to accidentally make it sound like we're Christians *because* we do good stuff. If we're talking to people about why we live as we do, we need to make sure our focus is on how God has changed us and made us people who bear good fruit.

Spend some time thinking about what you would say to someone who commented on the fact that you seem to live differently to others.

CHAPTER 12

You Are... A Fellow Suffering

^{12}Beloved, do not be surprised at the fiery trial when it comes upon you to test you, as though something strange were happening to you. ^{13}But rejoice insofar as you share Christ's sufferings, that you may also rejoice and be glad when his glory is revealed. ^{14}If you are insulted for the name of Christ, you are blessed, because the Spirit of glory and of God rests upon you. ^{15}But let none of you suffer as a murderer or a thief or an evildoer or as a meddler. ^{16}Yet if anyone suffers as a Christian, let him not be ashamed, but let him glorify God in that name. ^{17}For it is time for judgment to begin at the household of God; and if it begins with us, what will be the outcome for those who do not obey the gospel of God? ^{18}And "If the righteous is scarcely saved, what will become of the ungodly and the sinner?" ^{19}Therefore let those who suffer according to God's will entrust their souls to a faithful Creator while doing good.

1 Peter 4:12-19

Nothing Changes

Persecution isn't new. Christians have been persecuted since the very start of the Church.[a] In the first century, when the New Testament was written, there was no organised persecution by the Roman Empire. The famous examples of Christians being thrown to the lions didn't start till a bit later. But from its earliest days the Church experienced persecution on a less organised level. In the Roman Empire the Jews (physical descendants of God's chosen people in the Old Testament) had been given special permission to follow their religion even when it stopped them doing some of the things usually required of those in the Empire. While the Romans saw Christianity as just a type of Judaism it was relatively safe, but the more it became distinct from Judaism the more the Christians began to get in trouble. They were no longer protected by the special rules laid out for the Jews. Most persecution arose from misunderstandings about the Christians. They were accused of being cannibals because of misunderstandings about the Lord's Supper and of committing incest because they referred to each other as brothers and sisters.

Don't Be Surprised

As 21st-century Westerners our response to persecution is normally to object that such treatment goes against our human rights. We feel certain that this is something that shouldn't happen. Yet Peter tells the believers to whom he is writing, 'Do not be surprised at the fiery trial when it comes upon you' (1 Peter

---

[a] To be persecuted is to be mistreated, through words or actions, because of your personal beliefs. In this context, it is the unfair, negative treatment of Christians because of their beliefs about God and the Gospel.

4:12). Suffering is an inevitable part of being a Christian (Matthew 10:24-25; Romans 8:17). When Peter calls it 'the fiery trial' he's evoking biblical ideas about God refining his people, as if by a refining fire. To refine something is to remove its impurities. Engineers sometimes use fire to refine metals. The heat of the fire destroys the impurities which have got mixed in with the precious core metal. Peter used the same idea at the beginning of his letter: 'You may have had to suffer grief in all kinds of trials. These have come so that the proven genuineness of your faith – of greater worth than gold, which perishes even though refined by fire – may result in praise, glory and honour when Jesus Christ is revealed' (1 Peter 1:6-7 NIV). Persecution and suffering are not 'something strange' happening to you but part of God's purpose for you.

Therefore, rather than panicking or objecting when persecution comes, we should in fact rejoice because we are sharing in the sufferings of Christ (1 Peter 4:13). When we are persecuted we follow in the footsteps of Jesus. In Acts we are told that the apostles rejoiced 'that they were counted worthy to suffer dishonor for the name [i.e. Christ]' (Acts 5:41). We also rejoice because we know that if we endure suffering and persecution we will rejoice even more and be glad 'when [Jesus'] glory is revealed' (1 Peter 4:13), that is when he returns and brings in his perfect new creation.

All of this sounds a lot like Jesus who told his followers, 'Blessed are those who are persecuted because of righteousness, for theirs is the kingdom of heaven. Blessed are you when people insult you, persecute you and falsely say all kinds of evil against you because of me. Rejoice and be glad, because great is your reward in heaven' (Matthew 5:10-12 NIV). We are able to rejoice in present persecution when we remember that our reward is in heaven.

Don't Be Misunderstood

To be persecuted for belief in Christ is a sign that 'the Spirit of glory and of God rests upon you' (1 Peter 4:14). The 'Spirit of glory' is just another way of talking about the Holy Spirit, but because it includes a word Peter has just used to talk about that future day when Jesus returns, it also evokes ideas of that new creation breaking in. Those who are persecuted can be seen as blessed because their suffering proves that the Holy Spirit is in them. It proves they are true believers.

However, Peter quickly adds a condition to this. 'But let none of you suffer as a murderer or a thief or an evildoer or as a meddler' (1 Peter 4:15). To suffer for belief in Jesus is honourable, but to suffer – rightly or wrongly – for a crime like murder or theft or just for being a meddler (someone who is trying to control the morality of people outside of the Church) is dishonourable to God. Christians are God's representatives on earth – his living, breathing, walking temples. If we are seen as criminals, God's name is dishonoured. We are God's representatives and we need to take that seriously. Not all suffering is good suffering, for us or for God. We need to be above reproach, meaning that we are so far away from such wrongdoing that we can't even be accused of it. Peter is clear that bringing persecution upon ourselves by doing wrong is not a sign of blessing or a sign that God is living in us.

The title 'Christian' was first coined in Antioch, almost certainly by those outside of the Church as a negative term (Acts 11:26), so it is quite possible that many of those to whom Peter was writing had literally suffered 'as a Christian' (1 Peter 4:16).

Peter says this isn't a reason to be ashamed in itself but that these believers must 'glorify God in that name' (1 Peter 4:16). They must show that contrary to what many people believe, the Christians are not criminals and not a threat to their society. To be recognised as different, even as posing a challenge to people from God, is good. To dishonour God by associating him with wrong conduct is not.

Today, in the West, it isn't very common for people to assume that Christians are criminals, but it is still just as important that we make sure we are being good representatives for God, showing people what he's really like. In the same way that your impression of what teachers or dentists are like is probably formed more by your own experience of them than anything you've been told, so the impression most people have of Christians will be formed much more by the Christians they meet than by anything else. If we are known as the office gossip or someone who has a foul mouth or who looks at young women inappropriately, we are dishonouring God and not displaying what a Christian really should be. Just like those early believers Peter was writing to, we need to 'glorify God' in the name 'Christian'.

Understanding The Bigger Picture

Why do persecution and suffering happen? Because 'it is time for judgment to begin at the household of God' (1 Peter 4:17). God is judge. He will judge the living and the dead (1 Peter 4:5). There is no doubt in Peter's mind that Christians (those in 'the household of God') will be saved. As we've already seen, to be a Christian is to be 'in Christ', and that is an irreversible thing. But God is even now judging us, using suffering and persecution to refine us and make us more like the people he wants us to be. This doesn't mean that anyone who is suffering or being persecuted must secretly be a really bad Christian. This side of the new creation we are all on a lifelong journey of becoming more and more like the men and women God made us to be. Even Paul could be afflicted with a thorn in the flesh which was from God, for a purpose (2 Corinthians 12:7-10). He declared, 'For Christ's sake, I delight in weaknesses, in insults, in hardships, in persecutions, in difficulties. For when I am weak, then I am strong' (2 Corinthians 12:10 NIV).

We may think this is all a bit unfair and protest about it, but the reality is that we're the lucky ones. Peter quotes a proverb: 'If the righteous is scarcely saved, what will become of the ungodly and the sinner?' (1 Peter 4:18, quoting Proverbs 11:31). What we experience when we are persecuted is the tender discipline of a loving father, designed to do us good (Hebrews 12:6). If we, as loved children, receive this discipline, how much worse will things be for those who have rejected God?

Entrust Your Soul

We should rejoice in suffering, then, when it's 'according to God's will' (1 Peter 4:19). What should we do when we face these situations? We should entrust our souls 'to a faithful Creator while doing good' (1 Peter 4:19). If suffering is ultimately the good purpose of God for us, the best thing for us to do is to entrust ourselves to his wisdom and his care. God knows best and he is a loving father who wants to do what is best for us. While we do this we should also be looking to do good. Then, far from being persecuted for wrongdoing, we will stand as witnesses to the goodness of God.

Facing suffering and persecution is not easy but it is necessary. All Christians will face persecution and suffering of some sort. It is our responsibility to make sure that the persecution we face is not of our own making, in a way that dishonours God. Rather, when we suffer for the name of Christ, we are blessed, we can rejoice and look forward to the revelation of the glory of Jesus at his return, when all pain and suffering will cease.

> After you have suffered a little while, the God of all grace, who has called you to his eternal glory in Christ, will himself restore, confirm, strengthen, and establish you. To him be the dominion forever and ever. Amen.
>
> 1 Peter 5:10-11

Identity Check-Up

Here are some questions and activities to help you perform an identity check-up.

Understanding Your Identity

Read 1 Peter 4:12-19 and think about these questions.
- What reasons does Peter give us to rejoice when we suffer persecution? (vv.13-14)
- What is our role in persecution? What must we avoid? (vv.15-17)
- How does Peter view persecution within God's plan for the world? (vv.17-19 – See also 1 Peter 1:6-7)

Living Your Identity

Take some time to think about these questions or discuss them with others.

- Are there times when you have felt persecuted for your faith? What is your usual reaction?
- Do you find it easy to rejoice in these times? What do we need to do to help us to rejoice while suffering?
- Do you think of yourself as a representative for God? Is your life a good representation of what God is like?

Growing In Your Identity

Rejoicing in suffering can be very hard. It often doesn't come naturally! We will find it easier to rejoice when suffering if we are soaked in the truths which Peter points us to in this passage.

Write a paragraph or some bullet points outlining the reasons we have to rejoice when we are persecuted. Keep it somewhere safe, ready to read and encourage yourself when you are feeling persecuted.

CHAPTER 13

You Are... More Than A Conqueror

^{28}And we know that for those who love God all things work together for good, for those who are called according to his purpose. ^{29}For those whom he foreknew he also predestined to be conformed to the image of his Son, in order that he might be the firstborn among many brothers. ^{30}And those whom he predestined he also called, and those whom he called he also justified, and those whom he justified he also glorified.

^{31}What then shall we say to these things? If God is for us, who can be against us? ^{32}He who did not spare his own Son but gave him up for us all, how will he not also with him graciously give us all things? ^{33}Who shall bring any charge against God's elect? It is God who justifies. ^{34}Who is to condemn? Christ Jesus is the one who died—more than that, who was raised—who is at the right hand of God, who indeed is interceding for us. ^{35}Who shall separate us from the love of Christ? Shall tribulation, or distress, or persecution, or famine, or nakedness, or danger, or sword? ^{36}As it *is written, "For your sake we are being killed all the day long; we are regarded as sheep to be slaughtered."* [37]*No, in all these things we are more than conquerors through him who loved us.* [38]*For I am sure that neither death nor life, nor angels nor rulers, nor things present nor things to come, nor powers,* [39]*nor height nor depth, nor anything else in all creation, will be able to separate us from the love of God in Christ Jesus our Lord.*

Romans 8:28-39

Joseph And The Amazing Goodness Of God

The first book of the Bible contains the story of one of my favourite biblical characters: Joseph (Genesis 37-50). Joseph is the ultimate example of enduring unfair treatment at the hands of others while trusting in God. But what I love even more about the story is what it shows us about God.

Joseph had a rough time. First his brothers sell him into slavery. Then he's framed by Potiphar's wife and thrown into prison. He probably spent a total of 11 years as a slave and prisoner, and all for getting a little bit big-headed with his brothers and for standing his ground against the advances of Potiphar's wife. But when God starts to use him to interpret dreams, he's taken out of prison and becomes second-in-command in Egypt, organising a massive rationing system. So when his family are almost dying because of the famine, he's able to help them with supplies from the storehouses.

The pinnacle of the story is Joseph's assessment of everything that's happened to him. When his brothers are worried about what he's going to do to them after their father's death, this is what Joseph says to them: 'You meant evil against me, but God meant it for good, to bring it about that many people should be kept alive' (Genesis 50:20). Through all that had happened, Joseph knew that God had been in control and had been working out his good purpose even when things seemed awful. Joseph knew something about God which sustained him through years of unjust treatment. Thousands of years later, Paul, who was also treated unfairly by his kinsmen and thrown into prison more than once, wrote about the same idea.

Looking Under The Bonnet

Romans 8:28 is probably one of the best known and best loved verses in the Bible. Paul has been discussing suffering and the fact that we live in the tension of being in a world full of imperfections while we eagerly await God's promised new creation (Romans 8:18-25). He then tells us the fantastic truth that in times when we feel weak and don't even know what to pray, God's Spirit helps us to pray (Romans 8:26-27). It's at this point that Paul introduces the awesome promise that 'for those who love God all things work together for good, for those who are called according to his purpose' (Roman 8:28).

This promise is like taking a look under the bonnet. Imagine your car starts making a funny noise. You take it to a garage to get a professional to take a look. They open up the bonnet, give it a good look over and do some tests before assuring you that everything is working fine. Despite how things might seem on the outside, on the inside everything is working as it should. This promise gives us God's expert opinion as he opens the bonnet of our lives to show us what's going on. Though on the outside things may be scary and painful, the truth is that underneath it all God is in charge and he is making sure that all things work together for our good.

There's no promise here that life will be easy as a Christian. We've already seen that the New Testament actually promises us the exact opposite (e.g. Romans 8:17). But there is a promise that even in the most difficult times and terrible situations God is still in control and God is still good. The good promised here probably has two senses. First it has the sense of bringing us good in this life, even out of seemingly bad situations. God can use difficulty and suffering to shape us to be more like the people he designed us to be. Suffering helps us remember that we need God. It helps us to understand that God's grace is sufficient for us and his power is made perfect in our weakness (2 Corinthians 12:9). For two millennia Christians have testified to the fact that it is often through the hardest times in their lives that they have most grown in their relationship with God. Suffering is an invitation to intimacy and dependence on God. Whatever happens to us, God will use it for good.

The second sense in the use of 'good' in this promise is that everything is working towards that glorious day when God makes a new heavens and new earth and we will live with him for eternity (Revelation 21:1-22:5). This has been Paul's theme in the preceding verses. It's the ultimate good we are headed for, a destination God is preparing us for in everything we face.

Prove It!

But how can we know this for sure, and how can we help ourselves know this promise is true when life seems to be falling apart around us? Paul has an answer. To really *know* that God is always working for good we have to look at what he's already done for us. That's exactly what he goes on to do: he gives us a long list of the amazing blessings God has poured out on us, many of which we've already looked at. The whole list is introduced by the little word 'For' (Romans 8:29). The word Paul chooses indicates that what he's going to say explains and supports what he's just said. If we want to be sure that God is working all things together for good, we need to understand what Paul goes on to tell us.

First he says 'those whom he foreknew he also predestined'. The word 'foreknow' normally means 'to know something in advance'. But that doesn't really work here. That would imply that God looks down through history and sees something special about Christians. But not only does that completely contradict what the rest of the Bible says (see *You Are... Chosen*), it also fails to make sense of what Paul writes. He doesn't say that God foreknew our faith or our goodness, just that he foreknew us. This is a personal thing. It seems that Paul is actually using the word 'know' in a way found very often in the Old Testament, where 'to know' someone is about choosing and being in personal relationship with them.[a] So for God to foreknow us is for him to love us in advance and choose us.

The next step in the chain is that those foreknown are predestined. As we saw in *You Are... Chosen*, to predestine is to make a set decision in advance. Once God had loved us in advance

---

a The Hebrew word is *yāda*. E.g. Genesis 18:19 'For I have chosen [*yāda*] him...'; Jeremiah 1:5 'Before I formed you in the womb I knew [*yāda*] you, and before you were born I consecrated you' ('knew' and 'consecrated' are in parallel, implying a very similar meaning); Amos 3:2 'You only have I chosen [*yāda*] of all the families of the earth' (NIV). The Greek word Paul uses in Romans 8:29 is *proginōskō* which contains the word *ginōskō* used for *yāda* when the Old Testament was translated into Greek. Paul uses the same word in Romans 11:2.

and chosen us, he then made a set decision about the way the course of our lives would go.

What was this decision? It was that we would be 'conformed to the image of his Son, in order that he might be the firstborn among many brothers' (Romans 8:29). God predestined us to be made like Jesus. Human beings were made 'in the image of God' (Genesis 1:27). Now, in Christ we are being conformed to the image of God, in the shape of the image of Jesus. All this is so Jesus might be the first of many brothers. God predestined us to be in his family (as we saw in *You Are... Adopted*). We are sons of God and brothers of Jesus. That's what God decided in advance would be our lot.

The sequence continues in verse 30: 'And those whom he predestined he also called.' When Paul talks about someone being called he isn't just talking about hearing the Gospel somewhere, but having God work in us so that when we hear that Gospel we go from being spiritually dead to spiritually alive and respond in faith.[b] It's not like calling your dog, who may or may not choose to listen and come back to you. This is a call which both invites the hearer and evokes a response. This doesn't mean we don't need to keep telling people the Gospel; it means that when we do, it is God who awakens their hearts so they can respond, just as he did for us. All whom God has foreknown and predestined will hear and respond to his call.

Those called are 'also justified'. To be justified is to be put in a right legal standing with God. It is to have the declaration of 'no condemnation' spoken over us, as we saw in *You Are... Free From Condemnation*.

---

b E.g. Romans 9:24; 1 Corinthians 1:9; 7:17-22; Ephesians 4:1; 1 Thessalonians 2:1. See also 1 Thessalonians 1:4-5.

Finally in this sequence, those who are justified are 'also glorified'. Glorification is about our eternal destiny. One day God will transform both our bodies and this broken world to be perfect again, reflecting his glory. This is a theme Paul has already mentioned several times in this chapter: 'For I consider that the sufferings of this present time are not worth comparing with the glory that is to be revealed to us' (Romans 8:18). You might have noticed that Paul uses a past tense verb even though our glorification is a future blessing. He probably does this to emphasise its certainty. It is so certain that we will be glorified that he can talk about it as if it has already taken place, just like some of the Old Testament prophets do when they talk about future events (e.g. Isaiah 53).

So how can we *know* that God ensures all things work together for the good of those who love him? Because he's already foreknown us, then predestined us, then called us, justified us and given us a guarantee of future glory. It's God's acts of unbelievable love in all the spiritual blessings we've been exploring in this book that make us sure that he is good and that he is working for our good. So next time you're doubting God's goodness, take some time to think about these Gospel truths and see what that does for you.

What Then Shall We Say?

'What then shall we say to these things?' (Romans 8:31). What would you say? How does it feel knowing that God foreknew you and predestined you and called you and justified you and will one day glorify you? It's the kind of truth that could leave you speechless, but in Romans 8 Paul's got one more big point he wants us to get from it all: all of this guarantees beyond a doubt that nothing will ever be able to separate us from the love of God (Romans 8:39).

'If God is for us, who can be against us?' (Romans 8:31). In what may be the understatement of the millennium, Paul concludes that the great list of blessings we've read in verses 29-30 demonstrate that God is 'for us'. He loves us, wants good for us and wants to bless us. Now if *God* is for us, how can anyone else do us harm? People and powers might try to rage against us, but what hope do they have of success when we are secure as God's people, the recipients of all his blessings? And if this God has given up his very own Son for our sake, can there really be any other good thing he wouldn't give us? If someone laid on a giant banquet for you but when you sat down you found you didn't have a fork, would you feel nervous to ask for one or unsure that they would want to give you one? In the same way, if God has already given his son for us, anything else is a far smaller feat (Romans 8:32).

Paul continues to drive the point home by posing a load of challenges to this truth just to knock them all down so as to show the certainty of God's love and our security as his people. 'Who shall bring any charge against God's elect?' No one! Because God justifies (Romans 8:33) 'Who is to condemn?' No one! Because we are free from condemnation as those now 'in Christ', who died, was raised and now stands before God as our High Priest (Romans 8:34). Because of what Jesus did, no matter what anyone or anything tries to tell us, 'there is therefore now no condemnation' (Romans 8:1).

More Than Conquerors

'Who shall separate us from the love of Christ?' (Romans 8:35). Perhaps tribulation or persecution or danger or death? Nope. 'In

13. YOU ARE… MORE THAN A CONQUEROR • 153

all these things we are more than conquerors through him who loved us' (Romans 8:37). People in the ancient world knew about conquerors. Nations were always being taken over by other nations. Three centuries before Jesus, Alexander the Great had conquered a huge area. The empire he created actually didn't last very long but people felt its effects long afterwards. The Greek language and culture the conquerors imported was still shaping the lives of those at the time of Jesus and Paul. Closer to their day were the conquests of the Romans. The Christians Paul was writing to knew about this empire: they lived in the city which was at the very centre of it all.

Conquering is about being utterly victorious. No person or thing can stop a conqueror. We are 'more than conquerors'. Not only do we now conquer all of life's difficulties; each one is being worked together for good. We are now even greater than earthly conquerors all 'through him who loved us' (Romans 8:37). The word Paul uses here tells us that this loving was a one-time event; it refers to the cross where Jesus died, the ultimate demonstration of God's love for us (Romans 5:8; 1 John 3:16). Because Jesus died taking the punishment for sin and was raised to new life defeating death, nothing can stand against those who are in him.

All this leads Paul to one of the most awesome and powerful statements we find anywhere in the Bible. It's a statement built on the solid bedrock of the truth of what God has done in history through Jesus and what God has done in the lives of each and every Christian since. Everything we've looked at in these chapters helps us to join with Paul as he declares, 'I am sure that neither death nor life, nor angels nor rulers, nor things present nor things to come, nor powers, nor height nor depth, nor anything else in all creation, will be able to separate us from the love of God in Christ Jesus our Lord' (Romans 8:38-39).

Identity Check-Up

Here are some questions and activities to help you perform an identity check-up.

Understanding Your Identity

Read Romans 8:28-39 and think about these questions.
- Paul starts the promise of verse 28 with the words 'we know'. How do we know that all things work together for the good of those who love God?
- Verses 29-30 give us five things God has done for us. Can you summarise each in one sentence?
- What is a conqueror? What does it mean for us to be 'more than conquerors through him who loved us'? (v.37)

Living Your Identity

Take some time to think about these questions or discuss them with others.
- Do you think you really believe Romans 8:28 and 38-39? What stops you believing them?
- Given what Paul tells us about how we can *know* all things work together for good for those who love God, what should we do when we face difficulties and suffering?
- In what circumstances might you be tempted to feel you have been separated from the love of Christ? How can you remind yourself you haven't been?

Growing In Your Identity

We've seen that knowing the truth about what God has done for us is the real key to believing the promises of Romans 8:28 and 38-39. We need to keep reminding ourselves of these truths regularly by taking time to think, reflect and pray about them.

Create your own paragraph or list of sentences about the things God has already done for you through Jesus. You can write this in words, put it into pictures or even make a sound recording on your phone. They might be the things Paul reminds us of in this passage or they might be other elements of who we are which we've looked at as we've gone through the book. See how much you can get in there.

Spend some time thinking through each point. Reflect on what it means and then pray, thanking God for it and asking him to make it more and more real to you.

Stick your paragraph or list in your Bible or somewhere you'll see it and come back to it regularly, maybe every week, and do the same. Alternatively you might want to pick one or two of the points each time you take some time out to pray and read the Bible.

Whatever you do, keep reminding yourself of these truths. It's only then that you will really be able to say you *know* that 'for those who love God all things work together for good, for those who are called according to his purpose' (Romans 8:28).

Group Study Guides

These Group Study Guides have been written to help you use *Who In Heaven's Name Do You Think You Are?* as the basis for discussion in a group in which it is not assumed that everyone has read the relevant chapter. While brief notes are included to help you, it is assumed that the group leader has read the corresponding chapter before leading a discussion using one of these guides.

How To Use These Guides

The Group Study Guides follow the pattern of the *Identity Check-Up* provided for each chapter, focussing first on the biblical passage (*Understanding Your Identity*) and then on application to daily life (*Living Your Identity*). The questions in the second set are largely the same as those at the end of the relevant chapter, while the first section has been considerably expanded. You may also want to share the *Growing in Your Identity* activity from the corresponding chapter for people to do at some point on their own.

The guides are designed to be a starting point to help you as the discussion leader. In using them you will need to think about the people in your specific group and how you can best lead the discussion to help them. To get the most out of them, you should spend some time preparing before your group meets and be prepared to add things or change things to make it work for your context.

As well as the discussion questions, the guides include several elements designed to help you when leading a study. Each guide begins with a starter designed to get the group talking and thinking about a general point relevant to the topic. The starters include one or more questions and a statement of the key point to be drawn out which will be relevant to the passage being discussed.

Some discussion questions are followed by brackets which give the title in italics of a sub-section from the corresponding chapter where information particularly useful for that question can be found. Comments placed before a question are meant to introduce it or give some background. You will probably want to read these out to the group before asking the question. Comments which follow a question are to help you, as the leader, understand what the question is looking for so that, if necessary, you can help the group get to the right point. Where these comments are introduced by a phrase in italics, they refer specifically to the meaning of those words from the biblical text.

The guides are based on the *English Standard Version* but are also aware of the *New International Version* and the *New Living Translation*. Where these translations differ significantly and might bring confusion to the discussions a note is normally added below the relevant question.

Some Top Tips For Leading Group Discussions

Leading a good group discussion can be a hard task. Here are some tips to help you when using the *Who In Heaven's Name Do You*

Think You Are? study guides. They apply especially to the *Understanding Your Identity* questions but will hopefully also be useful in the *Living Your Identity* section.

1. Be prepared. Take some time to read the relevant chapter and then work through each question in the guide, noting the key points you want the discussion to draw out for each. Pray and ask God to help you, both in your preparation and in your leading of the discussion.

2. Before you begin, explain to the group the journey you'll be going on together: first seeking to understand the meaning of the biblical passage and then moving on to consider how it applies to our lives.

3. Use the starter question to get the group comfortable with sharing and thinking about the topic. Stress the key point given.

4. Encourage multiple people to answer each question. Once one person has said something, ask if anyone else wants to add something or agree or disagree. This will help avoid it becoming a quick-fire quiz.

5. Don't be afraid to question what people say or offer some guidance. You're not there to teach but there's no point in a discussion where everyone shares their opinion and no clear answer is ever reached. You don't want people leaving more confused than they were when they came!

Group Study Guide

1. You Are... Chosen

Starter

Key Point: Being chosen is a statement of value.
- Can you think of a time when you were chosen for something? How did being chosen make you feel?

Understanding Your Identity – *Ephesians 1:3-6*

In Ephesians 1:1-2 Paul opens his letter by introducing himself and then greeting the Christians who are in Ephesus. He then (vv.3-14) writes a great song of praise to God for all the spiritual blessings he has poured out on Christians.
- Why does Paul bless or praise God? (v.1) What do you think that means? (*Every Spiritual Blessing In Christ*)

- What does it mean to be 'in Christ'? (v.3)

In Christ: In Romans 5 Paul explains that God views all people as being in one of two groups. Each group has a figurehead, either Adam or Jesus. The people 'in Adam' (i.e. those who aren't Christians) receive what is due to Adam and those 'in Christ' (i.e. Christians) receive what is due to Christ. We don't deserve God's blessings, but because Jesus does we receive them through our union with him. (*Every Spiritual Blessing In Christ*)

- What is the first of the spiritual blessings with which we have been blessed? (v.4) What does this mean?

- What did God choose us for? (v.4 – *Chosen For A Purpose*)

- What is the second of the blessings we have received? (v.5) What does this mean? (*Chosen In Love For Adoption*)

- What does Paul conclude about God from the fact he has predestined us to be his sons?

In Love: Your group might have some different translations at the end of v.4 and beginning of v.5. The phrase 'in love' could be connected with what comes before it or what comes after. Some translations take it with v.4 (e.g. NLT, NKJV) but the majority attach it to v.5 (e.g. NIV, ESV, NASB), which is more likely to be correct.

We get a little more insight into why God chooses us in the Old Testament. In the book of Deuteronomy, Moses is talking to Israel, the people whom God had chosen to be his in the Old Testament, and he explains why God chose them.

- Read Deuteronomy 7:6-8. What does this tell us about why God chose to love us?

- What is the ultimate reason for God choosing us? (vv.5-6 – *To the Praise Of His Glorious Grace*)

Living Your Identity

- Paul's song tells us that God chose us and made his plan for us with the ultimate goal that he would be worshipped. How does this differ from what you might have previously thought?

- How does knowing God chose you make you feel?

- How does Paul respond to the truth that we are chosen by God? What can we learn from the way he responds?

- What impact should this truth make in our lives day by day? How can we help it make a difference to us?

GROUP STUDY GUIDE

2. You Are... A New Creation

Starter

Key Point: A new creation is something that has been completely transformed, not just tidied up.
- What ideas does the phrase 'a new creation' evoke for you?

You might want to share the *Extreme Makeover* illustration from *An Extreme Makeover*.

Understanding Your Identity – *2 Corinthians 5:14-17*

In the first sections of 2 Corinthians Paul is defending his position as an Apostle against criticism which has come to him from the church in Corinth, probably because false teachers had been misleading the Christians there. In our passage he is showing the Corinthians that everything he does is motivated by his desire to serve Christ, whatever others might have told them.
- What is it that motivates Paul in all he does? (v.14 – *A Change In View And A Change In State*)

- What are the consequences of the change in understanding Paul has had? (vv.16-17)

- What does it mean to look at something 'according to the flesh' (ESV) or 'from a worldly point of view' (NIV)? What is the alternative? (v.16)

Paul says that one of the things he sees from his new spiritual outlook is that all Christians are a 'new creation'. This phrase picks up a key idea from the Bible's big story. Take a look at these passages and think about the questions to help flesh out what the phrase 'new creation' means. (*New Creation*)

Genesis 2:5-9, 15-17

- What was life meant to look like for humans in God's original plan? Where were we designed to live and what was our relationship with God like?

Genesis 3:14-24

The serpent makes Eve question what God had said, and she and Adam eat from the tree of the knowledge of good and evil, the one tree from which God had told them not to eat. These verses tell us God's response.

- What is the situation of humans after the sin of Adam and Eve? What happened to the created world? (vv.17-19)

Isaiah 65:17-25

In this chapter the prophet Isaiah brings a message from God in which he warns the people that God will soon judge them because of their rebellion but also promises them that he will then bring salvation and will rescue them. These verses are part of God's promises to his people.

- What does God promise through Isaiah?

- If the culmination of God's plan for history is a new creation, what is the significance of Paul telling us that we are new creations? (2 Corinthians 5:17)

Living Your Identity

- What does the idea of being a 'new creation' tell us about what it means to be a Christian? (*Seeing It The Way God Does*)

- Is this how you tend to think of what happened to you when you became a Christian? If not, why not?

- How does being a 'new creation' shape our view of the future?

- How can we live in the light of this truth each day?

GROUP STUDY GUIDE

3. You Are... Free From Condemnation

Starter

Key Point: Sometimes a whole group of people receive the results of the actions of one individual, whether good or bad.

- When in your life have you been part of a group that has received the results of someone else's actions?

You might want to share the school class illustration from *One For All*.

Understanding Your Identity – *Romans 8:1 & 5:12-19*

Paul wrote his letter to the church in Rome in order to introduce to them both himself and the truth he preached, in the hope that he would soon be able to visit them and that they would help him on his mission to Spain (see Romans 1:11-15; 15:22-24). Romans gives us a great insight into some of the elements of the gospel which Paul preached.

- What is 'condemnation'? You might want to look at Romans 1:18 and 3:23. (*It All Goes Wrong*)

- Read Romans 8:1. Who is this talking about, what is it talking about and when is it talking about? (*No Condemnation*)

In Christ Jesus: God views all people as being in one of two groups. Each group has a figurehead, either Adam or Jesus. The people 'in Adam' (i.e. those who aren't Christians) receive what is due to Adam, and those 'in Christ' (i.e. Christians) receive what is due to Christ. We don't deserve God's blessings but because Jesus does we receive them through our union with him. (*Adam and Christ*)

What Paul says in Romans 8:1 all depends on what has come before. The word 'therefore' indicates that he can make this amazing statement because of what he's already said. We need to understand something of the previous chapters to really *know* that there is no condemnation for us as Christians.

Romans 5:12-19 is where Paul explains this idea of being 'in Christ' in more detail and shows how it means we can know we are free from condemnation. The passage can be divided into three sections.

Adam and Christ Introduced (Romans 5:12-14)

- Paul says that sin and death entered the world through one man and that death spread because 'all sinned', a phrase he explains in vv.13-14. What does it mean?

All sinned: This doesn't mean that all humans who followed Adam did things wrong (though that would also be true) but that God considered us all as sinners because of Adam's sin. Here is that idea of the actions of one affecting the many. Paul proves this in vv.13-14 by observing that sin couldn't be measured before the law was given, yet the fact that people still died showed they must have been sinners. Therefore, they must have been considered sinners because of what Adam did.

- What does it mean to say Adam was a 'type' (ESV) or 'pattern' (NIV) of Jesus? (v.14)

Adam and Christ Contrasted (Romans 5:15-17)

Even though he is going to show a comparison between Adam and Christ, Paul is very eager to show that there are some important differences too. He doesn't want people to misunderstand him and fail to see how much better Jesus is!

- What are the three big contrasts Paul draws between Adam and Christ? (vv.15-17)

Adam and Christ Compared (Romans 5:18-19)

Paul finally finishes the comparison he started in v.12 and makes his big point about the two groups they represent.

- What do we get from being 'in Adam'? What do we get from being 'in Christ'?

It is by being 'in Christ', as all Christians are, that we can *know* we are free from condemnation. Being placed in Christ's group is an irreversible event. And so when we do stuff wrong, God no longer sees that but sees Christ's perfect obedience and credits it to us.

Living Your Identity

- Do you really believe that you are no longer under condemnation? How do you feel when you slip up and sin?

- How can you fight against feeling condemned? What can you build into your life to make sure you enjoy this freedom?

- How does this truth challenge and change the way you think about God and your relationship with him?

- What should be our response to this truth?

GROUP STUDY GUIDE

4. You Are... Dead To Sin And Alive To God

Starter

Key Point: True freedom is the freedom to be who we were made to be.
- How would you define 'true freedom'?
- *Or* When do you feel most free?

You might want to share the pet fish illustration from *Understanding True Freedom*.

Understanding Your Identity – *Romans 6:1-23*

Paul wrote his letter to the church in Rome in order to introduce to them both himself and the truth he preached, in the hope he would soon be able to visit them and that they would help him on his mission to Spain (see Romans 1:11-15; 15:22-24). Romans gives us a great insight into some of the elements of the gospel which Paul preached.

In the previous chapters Paul has explained that if we are 'in Christ' we are free from condemnation for the things we have done wrong. In this passage Paul responds to misunderstandings this might have caused among his readers.

- What are the two misunderstandings Paul is addressing? (vv.1, 15)

Paul responds by explaining in more detail what happened when we became Christians.

- How does he describe our situation in relation to sin before we became Christians? (e.g. vv.6, 16-17, 20-21 – *Dying With Christ And Dying To Sin*)

- How and why does this situation change when we become Christians? (vv.2-11, 17-18, 22)

Here the idea of union with Christ is once again central. Because we are 'in Christ' our old self, which was enslaved to sin, has died with Christ on the cross, and because Christ rose from the dead we have been given the power to live a new life, no longer enslaved to sin but alive to God.

- What does it mean to 'consider' (ESV), 'count' (NIV) or 'reckon' (KJV) yourselves 'dead to sin and alive to God'? (v.11)

You might want to use the illustration from *Consider Yourselves...*

In the second half of the passage Paul uses the illustration of two different types of slavery to make the same point.

- What does the idea of slavery say about the nature of these relationships? How do a slave and their master interact? (*Freedom In Slavery*)

Paul tells us that we have been set free from slavery to sin (vv.17-18) but he doesn't say that we are now free people, without a master.

- Who or what are we now enslaved to? (vv.18, 22)

- What does this tell us about true freedom?

The point here is that we become free by being enslaved to righteousness and to God. True freedom is not the freedom to go and do whatever we like but to live in conformity with God's design for human behaviour. We experience true freedom and contentment when we live God's way.

Living Your Identity

- 'If there's no condemnation for me because I'm "in Christ" I can keep doing what I like. It makes no difference.' How would you respond to a friend who said this to you?

- Why is it important that we really understand what true freedom is?

- What can we do to get this truth deeply embedded in us and how can we use it to fight temptation?

- How should the combination of this study and the previous study (*You Are... Free From Condemnation*) shape the way we respond to and seek to help a Christian who comes to us and confesses they are struggling with repeated sin?

GROUP STUDY GUIDE

5. You Are... Dead To The Law

Starter

Key Point: Laws are for the living.
- What are laws for? Who are they given to?

You might want to share the story from *Dead Men Being Executed?*

Understanding Your Identity – *Romans 7:1-6*

Paul wrote his letter to the church in Rome in order to introduce to them both himself and the truth he preached, in the hope he would soon be able to visit them and that they would help him on his mission to Spain (see Romans 1:11-15; 15:22-24). Romans gives us a great insight into some of the elements of the gospel which Paul preached.

Having addressed possible misunderstandings of his teaching about the status of Christians as those 'in Christ', Paul now turns to discuss the place of the Old Testament law for those 'in Christ'.
- What is the general statement of fact on which Paul's argument relies? (v.1 – *Laws For The Living*)

- In what way does the marriage relationship illustrate this point? (vv.2-3)

- What set of laws is Paul particularly thinking about here?

Law: In this context, 'the law' means the commandments given to Israel in the Old Testament. The law was given by God as part of a covenant, a relationship in which each party had a clear role. Israel had to keep the law in order to receive God's blessing. If they failed to keep the law God would judge them, as happened when the Assyrians and Babylonians invaded them and took them into exile.

- How does this principle apply to our relationship to the Old Testament law? (vv.4, 6 – *Dying To The Law*)

You might want to use the soldier illustration from *Dying To The Law*.

- What was the purpose of our dying to the law? (v.4b – *A New Way To Live*)

- What does the image of fruit bearing suggest about the new way we live by God's standards?

Fruit trees don't have to strive to produce fruit; it's something that comes naturally to them when they are given the right conditions. Living by laws encourages us to strive to be good, but bearing fruit is a natural process. The next question looks at how that is possible.

- If we don't live by the law, how do we seek to live in the way God wants us to? (v.6)

Living Your Identity

- What have you done or used in the past to try and help you live God's way? Did these things work?

- Are there any laws you have been living under (either because you put them there yourself or someone else forced them upon you) which have been making you feel condemned and stealing the freedom God has given you?

- What can we do to help ourselves live God's way? How should this play out in our lives each day?

Group Study Guide

6. You Are... Adopted

Starter

Key Point: Real adoption is about relationship and security.

- These days you can adopt just about anything. Can you think of some examples? What is the difference between these and real adoption?

You might want to use some of the examples in *'I've Adopted A...'*

Understanding Your Identity – *Romans 8:14-17*

Paul wrote his letter to the church in Rome in order to introduce to them both himself and the truth he preached, in the hope he would soon be able to visit them and that they would help him on his mission to Spain (see Romans 1:11-15; 15:22-24). Romans gives us a great insight into some of the elements of the gospel which Paul preached.

In Romans 8, having looked at the blessings of being 'in Christ' which we have explored in the last few studies, Paul talks about the Christian life as a life lived with the Holy Spirit and about the Christian hope for the future.

- Who receives the blessing of being adopted as God's sons? (v.15 – See also Romans 8:9)

All who are led by the Spirit: This refers to Christians. Paul has just told us that all Christians have some measure of the Holy Spirit (see Romans 8:9). It doesn't mean a special group of Christians who are good at consciously letting the Spirit lead them.

- How do we become 'sons of God'? (v.15)

Adoption: On adoption in New Testament times see the last paragraph of *The Spirit Of Adoption As Sons.*

- What are the three differences that being adopted makes to our lives? (vv.15-17 – *Living As Sons*)

- What are we destined to inherit as heirs of God? (See Romans 8:20-25)

- What is the last, rather surprising, consequence of being a son of God? (v.17)

Living Your Identity

- What images and associations does the idea of God as father create in your mind?

- To what extent does your position as a son who has received the Spirit of adoption affect your life at the moment? Is this an aspect of your identity you regularly think about?

- How should being adopted by God affect our lives?

- What does or could get in the way of living in your position as a son and heir? What do you need to do to more actively live out your position as a son and heir of God?

Group Study Guide

7. You Are... A Witness

Starter

Key Point: Witnessing is simply reporting to others what you have seen or experienced.
- What do you associate with the idea of witnessing?
- *Or* What does it mean to be a witness in a law court?

Understanding Your Identity – *Luke 24:44-49 & Acts 1:6-11*

Luke's Gospel and Acts form a two-volume work which tell us about the life, death and resurrection of Jesus and the first few decades of the Church. There are lots of themes that tie the two volumes together, one of which is the idea of witnessing.

Comparing Luke's statements about witnessing in his gospel and Acts can help us better understand what Jesus meant when he commissioned us to be witnesses.

- What does Jesus mean when he tells the disciples they are 'witnesses of these things'? (Luke 24:48) What are the things of which they are witnesses? (*Being A Witness, Ready To Witness*)

- When Jesus is with the disciples a few weeks later he tells them, 'You will be my witnesses' (Acts 1:8). What does being a witness mean here?

- What does it mean to be a witness for Jesus, given what he says in Luke 24 and Acts 1?

Being a witness is a two-stage process, modelled in these two passages. First you become a witness by seeing or experiencing something yourself, then you act as a witness by reporting what you know to others. It is just like a witness in court who has become a witness by learning something about a crime and then acts as a witness by reporting those facts to the court.

- How does Jesus promise to help the disciples to be his witnesses? (Luke 24:49; Acts 1:8 – *You Will Receive Power*)

- Where does Jesus want his witnesses to go? (Acts 1:8 – *To The End Of The Earth...*)

At this point, the disciples were in Jerusalem; Judea and Samaria were the wider areas to the south and north respectively and 'the end of the earth' probably meant the rest of the known world. Jesus was saying that they were to be witnesses everywhere!

Living Your Identity

- What does the idea of 'witnessing' mean to you? Have these passages challenged that?

- As 21st-century Christians we haven't seen Jesus like the original disciples had, but what have we witnessed which we can report to others?

- What does God offer us to help us be witnesses? How should we pursue that?

- Witnessing is always easier if we've thought about the kind of things we would tell someone before the moment comes. If you had a few minutes to witness to a friend or family member, what would you say?

GROUP STUDY GUIDE

8. You Are... A Member Of The Body Of Christ

Starter

Key Point: One body is made up of many parts, all of which are needed to work together to make the body function well.
- How many parts do you think one human body has?

Answer: According to the *Terminologia Anatomica* (which gives the official, internationally recognised terms for human anatomy) there are more than 7500 different parts in a human body.

You might want to remind people of the advert mentioned in *A Running Nose*.

Understanding Your Identity – *1 Corinthians 12:12-31*

1 Corinthians is a letter written by Paul to the church in Corinth. It addresses some issues in the church which Paul has heard about through the reports of others and a letter from the church.

In chapter 12 Paul is beginning to address questions the church have sent him about spiritual gifts (v.1).

- In vv.14-20 Paul makes two observations about the human body. What are they? (*One Body, Many Parts*)

- Verse 27 tells us that 'all of you are the body of Christ, each an individual part' (author's translation). The body of Christ is the Church. What does this tell us about what the Church is and isn't?

The Church is a group of people linked together by faith in Christ, not a building. We don't go to church; we are the Church. (*You Are The Body Of Christ*)

- What is God's role in the body of Christ? (vv.28-29 – *The Arrangement Of The Body*)

- What are some of the gifts Paul lists? (vv.28-30) What do you think they are?

- What is the point of the list of questions in v.29?

- What should our attitude towards spiritual gifts be? (v.31 – *Earnestly Desire*)

Higher gifts: The idea of higher gifts ('greater gifts' NIV; 'most helpful gifts' NLT) might seem a little out of place given what Paul has already said in these verses. The explanation comes in chapter 14 where Paul explains that prophecy is especially to be desired because it builds up the church (14:4), whereas a tongue needs to be accompanied by an interpretation to build up the church (14:5).

Living Your Identity

- Do you think of yourself as a vital part of the body of Christ? If not, why not?

- What impact should the truths in this passage have on our churches and on our relationships with others within our churches?

- What gifts do you feel God has given you, or do others recognise in you? Are you using them to play your part in the body?

- Do you earnestly desire the higher gifts? How can we grow in our use of the gifts?

GROUP STUDY GUIDE

9. You Are... A Temple Of The Holy Spirit

Starter

Key Point: Where you are affects how you act.
- When have you been somewhere which made you very conscious about how you acted? Why did the place have this effect on you?

You might want to use the example given in *Knowing Where You Are*.

Understanding Your Identity – *1 Corinthians 6:12-20*

1 Corinthians is a letter written by Paul to the church in Corinth which addresses some issues in the church which Paul has heard about through the reports of others and a letter from the church.

Chapters 5 and 6 of this letter address matters relating to the church which someone has reported to Paul ('It is actually reported...' 5:1). Chapter 5 deals with a specific case of sexual immorality in the church, while 6:1-11 addresses the issue of church members taking their disagreements to a secular court. In 6:12-20 Paul returns to the issue of sexual immorality.

Sexual immorality: In the Bible's terms, sexual immorality is any sexual act which takes place outside of a marriage relationship between a man and a woman. That means it covers incest, adultery, homosexual acts and lust (see Matthew 5:27-28). The word Paul uses is *porneia* from which we get the word 'pornography'.

- In v.12 Paul quotes a slogan that was probably being used to justify sinful behaviour in the church in Corinth. What is the slogan? Does Paul agree with it? What is his response? (*Lawful But Not Good*)

- Verse 13 gives another slogan and Paul's response. What is the slogan and how does Paul respond?

Paul now gives his 'Top 5 Reasons Why Christians Should Flee From Sexual Immorality'. (*5 Reasons To Flee From Sexual Immorality*)

- *Number 5*: What is Paul's first reason for not engaging in sexual immorality? (v.14)

- *Number 4:* Why does being a member of the body of Christ mean we should flee from sexual immorality? (vv.15-17)

- *Number 3:* What does it mean to say sexual immorality is committing a sin against our own bodies? (v.18)

- *Number 2:* What does it mean to be a 'temple of the Holy Spirit' and how does it relate to fleeing sexual immorality? (v.19)

Temple: A temple is the dwelling place of a god. The people of Corinth knew about temples because their city was home to two significant examples. In the Old Testament the living, creator God chose to dwell with his people, first in a tent (Exodus 40:34-38) and then in a permanent temple in Jerusalem (1 Kings 8:10-11). Because these buildings were the place where God dwelt and met with humans they were places of great holiness – i.e. set apart and completely incompatible with sin. Now, God chooses to make us his temples. If God is living in us, how can we let our bodies be involved in sexual immorality?

- *Number 1:* Why are we not our own? (vv.19b-20) How does this contrast with the view of contemporary culture?

Living Your Identity

- Do you ever say or think something similar to 'But all things are lawful for me'? What should we remind ourselves when we have these thoughts?

- How can we apply Paul's 'Top 5 Reasons Why Christians Should Flee Sexual Immorality' to our lives in practical ways? What sort of things do we need to do and constantly remind ourselves?

- What are the real danger areas in your life where you need to be on your guard and ready to flee sexual immorality?

- How does the truth of 1 Corinthians 6:11 encourage us in our battle against sexual immorality?

GROUP STUDY GUIDE

10. You Are... Part Of A Holy Priesthood

Starter

Key Point: Having 'Access All Areas' normally comes with responsibility.

- Have you ever been given an 'Access All Areas' pass? If so, why were you given it?
- *Or* Why might someone be given 'Access All Areas'?

Understanding Your Identity – *1 Peter 2:4-10*

Peter wrote this letter to Christians in five regions of the Roman Empire about 30 years after Jesus had returned to be with his father. It seems these Christians were experiencing some sort of opposition and Peter wrote to encourage them and instruct them how to live in this difficult situation.

- Who is the living stone and what happens when we come to him? (vv.4-5 – *A Spiritual House*)

Spiritual house: 'House' was another term that could be used for a temple (the dwelling place of a god) in the ancient world (e.g. 1 Kings 5:1-6; Luke 6:4).

Read Leviticus 9:1-7 (especially v.7), Exodus 19:22 and 1 Samuel 2:28.

- What were the privileges and role of the Old Testament priests?

Privileges: Access to God, through their service in the temple. *Role:* To act as the middlemen between God and Israel to allow them to communicate. To perform sacrifices which ensured the continuation of the relationship between Israel and God. (*Temples and Priests*)

- What privileges does our position as 'a holy priesthood' give us?

You might want to take a look at Hebrews 4:14, 16. (*Temples And Priests*)

- What responsibilities do we have as 'a holy priesthood'? How do we do this?

Spiritual sacrifices: This is a metaphorical reference to lots of things we do which are acts of worship. Take a look at Psalms 50:14; 51:17; 141:2; Hebrews 13:15-16; Romans 12:1. (*Playing A Role*)

Verse 9 gives us a list of four elements of our identity as Christians. Each is taken from the Old Testament (see Exodus 19:5-6; Deuteronomy 7:6; Isaiah 43:20-21), showing that

Christians stand in continuity with Israel, God's Old Testament people.

- What are the four things Peter says about us as Christians? What do they mean? (*Living As God's People*)

- What is the purpose of all this? (v.9b)

Proclaim the excellencies: The same word for 'proclaim' [*exangellō*] is used in the Greek translation of the Psalms where the idea is always about worship, not evangelism – e.g. Psalm 79:13 ('[We] will give thanks to you forever; from generation to generation we will recount [*exangellō*] your praise') and Psalm 107:22 ('And let them offer sacrifices of thanksgiving, and tell [*exangellō*] of his deeds in songs of joy!'). This means the proclaiming is almost certainly about worship, not evangelism. It is very similar to the idea of spiritual sacrifices in v.5. The translation of v.9 in the NLT ('you can show others the goodness of God') makes it sound as though evangelism is in mind and is probably misleading.

Living Your Identity

- Do you live as if you really have constant, direct access to God? How can we help ourselves live in light of this truth?

- Do you think of yourself as offering spiritual sacrifices to God and proclaiming his excellencies?

- How should our role as a holy priesthood affect our daily lives?

Group Study Guide

11. You Are... Salt And Light

Starter

Key Point: Christians have a role to play in preserving goodness in society and showing people what God is like.

- What examples can you think of where Christians have had a positive effect on society?

Understanding Your Identity – *Matthew 5:13-16*

Matthew chapters 5-8 are an account of Jesus teaching his followers on the side of a mountain, often called the Sermon on the Mount. He teaches them how they should live as those in God's kingdom on earth.

- Why do you think salt was so important in Jesus' day?

Whereas we use salt primarily to flavour our food, in the ancient world salt was most important as a preservative; it would be rubbed into meat to slow down the process of decay.

- If salt was primarily used as a preservative in Jesus' day, what does it mean for Christians to be 'the salt of the earth'? (v.13 – *Keep It Salty*)

- What does it mean to be 'the light of the world'? (vv.14-16 – *Let Your Light Shine*)

- How does Jesus use the example of a lamp to make his point? (v.15)

- What is the end goal of letting our light shine? (v.16)

Living Your Identity

- In what ways can we be salt in our day-to-day lives?

- What might stop us from fulfilling our role as 'the salt of the earth'?

- In what issues in modern society do Christians need to act as 'the salt of the earth'?

- How can we be lights in the world?

- What do we need to do to make sure our light isn't hidden?

GROUP STUDY GUIDE

12. You Are... A Fellow Sufferer

Starter

Key Point: All Christians will face persecution and suffering.

- When have you felt you were being persecuted or suffering?

Understanding Your Identity – *1 Peter 4:12-19*

Peter wrote this letter to Christians in five regions of the Roman Empire about 30 years after Jesus had returned to be with his father. It seems these Christians were experiencing some sort of opposition and Peter wrote to encourage them and instruct them how to live in this difficult situation.

- How does Peter encourage his readers to respond when the 'fiery trial' of persecution comes upon them? (vv.12-13 – *Don't Be Surprised*)

When his glory is revealed: This means when Jesus returns and God judges all people before we enter the new creation.

- Why does Peter say it is a good thing to be 'insulted for the name of Christ'? (vv.14-16 – *Don't Be Misunderstood*)

- What is the exception he gives to the value of being persecuted? (v.15)

Peter explains this situation by placing it in the bigger picture of what's going on.

- What is this bigger picture? (vv.17-18 – *Understanding The Bigger Picture*)

Persecution and suffering are the beginning of God's judgement, which starts with his people. However, Peter doesn't doubt that all Christians will be saved. For those of us 'in Christ' this judgement is part of God's quest to refine us, making us more like the people he wants us to be (see 1 Peter 1:6-7).

- What does Peter conclude that those who experience persecution and suffering should do? (v.19 – *Entrust Your Soul*)

Living Your Identity

- Are there times when you have felt persecuted for your faith? What was your reaction?

- Do you find it easy to rejoice in these times? What do we need to do to help us to rejoice while suffering?

- How can we avoid suffering for the wrong reasons?

- Do you think of yourself as a representative for God? Is your life a good representation of what God is like?

GROUP STUDY GUIDE

13. You Are... More Than A Conqueror

Starter

Key Point: Sometimes things can seem really bad on one level but are actually working towards a good end.
- When have you experienced something which you thought was a disaster but actually worked out for good?

Understanding Your Identity – *Romans 8:28-39*

Paul wrote his letter to the church in Rome in order to introduce to them both himself and the truth he preached, in the hope he would soon be able to visit them and that they would help him on his mission to Spain (see Romans 1:11-15; 15:22-24). Romans gives us a great insight into some of the elements of the gospel which Paul preached.

In Romans 8, having looked at the blessings of being 'in Christ' we explored in some of the earlier studies, Paul talks about the Christian life as a life lived with the Holy Spirit and about the Christian hope for the future.

Romans 8:28 is probably one of the best known and most loved verses in the Bible.

- What is the promise made in v.28? What do you think is the 'good' it mentions? (*Looking Under The Bonnet*)

All things work together for good: There is some minor variation between English translations of this phrase (e.g. ESV: 'all things work together for good'; NIV: 'in all things God works for the good...'). This is because of ambiguities about how the words in the original Greek relate to each other. The meaning is not in doubt: God is involved in the lives of his people and makes everything work towards his ultimate good, however things might seem on the surface.

The verses that follow show us how we can really know and be sure that this promise is true. They give us a sequence of five things God has done for us as Christians, many of which we've already looked at in these studies.

- What are the five things God has done for us and what do they mean? (vv.29-30 – *Prove It!*)

Foreknew: Here the idea of knowing is used in a way commonly found in the Old Testament, where it denotes the idea of choosing and loving someone. Loosely translated here it means 'loved in advance'.

Predestined: Making a set decision in advance.

Called: In the way Paul uses it this doesn't just mean hearing the Gospel but having God work in our hearts to evoke a response to him.

Justified: Means being put in a right legal standing before God, receiving the verdict 'not guilty'.

Glorified: Refers to our eternal destiny of being with God in a new creation and new resurrection bodies. Though it is in the past tense, it is actually a future event. The use of the past tense emphasises how certain it is.

- What is the conclusion Paul draws from these truths? How does he emphasise this point? (vv.31-36 – *What Then Shall We Say?*)

- What is a conqueror? What does it mean to be 'more than conquerors' and how do we perform this role? (v.37 – *More Than Conquerors*)

- What is Paul's final great conclusion to all he's been saying? (vv.38-39)

Living Your Identity

- Do you think you really believe Romans 8:28 and 38-39? What stops you believing them?

- Given what Paul tells us about how we can *know* all things work together for good for those who love God, what should we do when we face difficulties and suffering?

- In what circumstances might you be tempted to feel you have been separated from the love of Christ? How can you remind yourself you haven't been?

Printed in Great Britain
by Amazon